COUNTRY EMPLOYMENT POLICY REVIEW

DECENT WORK FOR ALL :

TARGETING FULL EMPLOYMENT IN THAILAND

INTERNATIONAL LABOUR OFFICE
East Asia Multidisciplinary Advisory Team
Bangkok Area Office

August 2000

ISBN 92-2-112354-5
August 2000

Printed in Thailand

Contents

Contents *(continued)*

Contents *(continued)*

Tables

Tables *(continued)*

Preface

It is now three years since the Asian financial crisis brought the spectre of unemployment vividly to life in East Asia. This report, *Decent work for all: Targeting full employment in Thailand*, presents a timely examination of the issues and challenges in tackling the employment situation in Thailand. It is one of a series of Country Employment Policy Reviews carried out as part of the ILO's work to follow up on the World Summit for Social Development, which accepted the centrality of employment in development strategies. This is all the more relevant in the present context where the ILO is focusing on the primary goal of promoting equal access to opportunities for decent work for women and men, in conditions of freedom, equity, security and human dignity.

This review is the second to be carried by the ILO in Asia. It offers useful insights into the complex relationship between economic development and the world of work – insights that are of direct relevance within both Thailand and other countries in the region.

Promoting opportunities for decent and productive work is the report's keynote theme. Carried out by a team of ILO specialists whose expertise ranges across a number of disciplines, it examines the critical elements of the world of work in Thailand today, and flags future directions and policy options. Important areas highlighted by the report include: macro-trends and employment implications; job-creation strategies, especially small enterprise development; social protection; skill development strategies; industrial relations; tripartism; and labour market information. In each area, the report has identified priority issues and made concrete proposals for improving policies and programmes. Gender issues and international labour standards are cross-cutting themes throughout the report.

Tripartism has been the hallmark of the review process – involving extensive consultations with government, employers' and workers' representatives at every stage. The ILO circulated a preliminary summary of findings and recommendations to tripartite constituents and received valuable comments which have helped shape the final version. A consultative workshop in October 1999 reviewed a draft of the Country Employment Policy Review, and feedback from the government and the social partners is reflected in the final report.

Particular acknowledgement must be given to the strong support and contributions made by the Ministry of Labour and Social Welfare at all stages, in particular by the Deputy Permanent Secretary, Mr. Kirasak Chancharaswat and the senior staff of all departments and offices of the Ministry. The social partners, through a number of employers' and workers' organizations, similarly made an important contribution to the report. The consultation process also included other government agencies and civil society, including non-governmental organizations (NGOs)and the academic world.

Within the ILO, the Country Employment Policy Review exercise was jointly led by Mr. William R. Simpson, the then Director of the East Asia Multidisciplinary Advisory Team (EASMAT), Bangkok and Mr. Ng Gek Boo, then Chief of the Employment and Labour Market Policies Branch, Employment and Training Department, Geneva. Mr. Rueben Dudley, Deputy Regional Director and Officer in Charge of EASMAT, oversaw work through the report's final stages.

Mr. Piyasiri Wickramasekara, Senior Specialist in Labour market Policies, ILO/EASMAT, acted as the overall coordinator of the Review and report, working together with a team of ILO specialists. The Bangkok Area Office, under the guidance of Deputy Director, Mr. Siwu Liu; Programme Officer responsible for Thailand, Mr. Pracha Vasuprasat; and EASMAT programme officer, Ms. Chomesri Vichitlekakarn provided valuable backstopping support.

This report should provide an important foundation for future work to improve employment policies in Thailand in the medium term. It may also offer food for thought for other countries which may face similar issues. It is, in a sense, a policy blueprint which can be used either in whole or in part. It can be used to guide national policies and programmes, and also in negotiations with donor agencies. This Country Employment Policy Review could provide an important foundation for further developing the programme of fruitful cooperation with tripartite partners in Thailand to ensure decent work opportunities for all.

Ian Chambers
Director
ILO Area Office and the
East Asia Multidisciplinary
Advisory Team

August 2000

Acknowledgements

Chapter 1, offering a macro-economic overview of the labour market and policy was prepared by Elizabeth Morris, Peter Richards, Moazam Mahmood and Piyasiri Wickramasekara. In Chapter 2, Gerry Finnegan and Simon White examine enterprise policies; Piyasiri Wickramasekara, job creation; and Phan Thuy, Don Fraser and Robert Heron, employment services. In Chapter 3, Anne Drouin, Kenneth Thompson and Pracha Vasuprasat consider social protection and unemployment benefits; in Chapter 4, Trevor Riordan and Anthony Twigger examine skill development in the context of growth, productivity and competitiveness. In Chapter 5, Duncan Campbell addresses social dialogue and employment issues. Chapter 6, by Elizabeth Morris, considers labour market information and policy. Chapter 7 summarizes the conclusions and recommendations of the report, and was prepared by Peter Richards and Piyasiri Wickramasekara. Cross-cutting themes were addressed by various specialists: international labour standards by Joachim Grimsmann; gender issues by Nelien Haspels; and workers' and employers' issues by Kimi Takagi, Raghwan Raghwan and Tan Peng Boo. Background papers were prepared by Sanajaya Lall and Sununta Siengthai. Technical editing was carried out by Gek-Boo Ng, Piyasiri Wickramasekara and Peter Richards; final editing for publication by Robert Few and initially by Penelope Ferguson and coordinated by Piyasiri Wickramasekara. Typesetting was performed by Pannipa Ratanawijarn, assisted by Naiyana Punnakitti.

Introduction

At the 1995 World Summit for Social Development, participating countries including Thailand made a commitment to "promoting the goal of full employment as a basic priority of ... economic and social policies, and to enabling all men and women to attain secure and sustainable livelihoods through freely chosen productive employment and work" (Commitment 3). The ILO has been given a special mandate by the UN system to assist countries in the fulfilment of this commitment. As a follow up to the World Summit, the ILO has been engaged in a series of Country Employment Policy Reviews (CEPRs) in various regions of the world.

It was in this context that the ILO contacted the Thai government and social partners regarding the possibility of a CEPR. Thailand presents a most interesting case both because it ratified the ILO's Employment Policy Convention, 1964 (No. 122), in 1969 and also because of its rapid growth leading to virtual full employment conditions by the early 1990s (although the 1997 economic crisis put a temporary brake on this rapid growth). Following a very positive response, the ILO conducted a CEPR in Thailand during 1998/99 with the full consent of the Royal Thai Government and the employers' and workers' organizations.

The terms of reference for the CEPR were developed in accordance with a series of consultations with various government agencies, representatives of employers' and workers' organizations and after research conducted by an ILO mission.[1] There was general agreement that the CEPR exercise would adopt a medium-term perspective and focus only on selected issues: job creation through enterprises, skills and competitiveness; social protection and social dialogue – all aimed at achieving decent work for all.

The technical work was carried out by the ILO East Asia Multidisciplinary Advisory Team (ILO/EASMAT), based in Bangkok, in collaboration with the ILO's Employment and Training Department, relevant units at headquarters, the Regional Office for Asia and the Pacific (ROAP) and the ILO Bangkok Area Office. In addition to ILO experts, several national and international consultants provided input. From the beginning, emphasis was placed on the CEPR process, which meant consultations with concerned agencies and partners at different stages. Interim findings on various issues were presented at briefings and workshops involving all concerned parties. The ILO organized four tripartite consultations as part of the CEPR process based on interim findings:

(i) Tripartite National Workshop on Training for Recovery: A Review of Training Policies, Programmes and Systems to Facilitate Economic Recovery, Amari Watergate Hotel, 17-18 March 1999.

(ii) Tripartite Consultation on the Labour Market Information System for Thailand, Royal Princess Hotel, 21 July 1999.

---

[1] The ILO mission consultations took place from 27 Oct. to 3 Nov. 1998. The mission consisted of W.R. Simpson, Director, ILO/EASMAT (Team Leader); Gek-Boo Ng, Chief, POLEMP, Geneva; Piyasiri Wickramasekara, Senior Specialist in Labour Market Policies, ILO/EASMAT; and Pracha Vasuprasat, Programme Officer, Bangkok Area Office.

(iii) Tripartite Consultation on Social Dialogue and Employment Policy Choices in Thailand, Royal Princess Hotel, 17 August 1999.

(iv) Tripartite Consultation on the Tentative Summary of Findings and Recommendations, Bangkok, 29 September – 1 October 1999.

These consultations were attended by social partners, concerned government agencies, the academic community and international agencies and donors. The meetings provided valuable feedback for preparation of the technical reports.

Following the completion of the main report, the ILO organized the National Tripartite Workshop on Country Employment Policy Review for Thailand, during 21-22 October 1999 in Cha-am. This was attended by senior officials of the Ministry of Labour and Social Welfare, other concerned government agencies, employers' and workers' organizations and academics. The final report has taken into account various concerns expressed at the meeting. It was also circulated at the ILO International Consultation concerning Follow-up to the World Summit for Social Development, held in Geneva in November.[2] The ILO in Bangkok is already following up on a number of recommendations made in the CEPR with the Ministry of Labour and Social Welfare, especially in the areas of social protection, labour market policies and labour market information.

The report is organized as follows. Chapter 1 traces macro-economic developments prior to the crisis, the current employment and labour market situation and issues and challenges. Chapter 2 deals with the critical area of job creation, especially the role of small enterprise development and social investments. Chapter 3 examines issues and options in social protection. Chapter 4 undertakes a review of skill development policy issues. Chapter 5 discusses social dialogue and its impact on employment choices. Chapter 6 reviews labour market information and areas for improvement. Chapter 7 synthesises the findings in various chapters and details appropriate policy implications.

---

[2] The International Labour Organization and the Promotion of Full, Productive and Freely Chosen Employment: International Consultation concerning Follow-up to the World Summit for Social Development, International Labour Office, Geneva, 2-4 November 1999.

Chapter 1

Macro-economic overview

This chapter reviews the main elements in Thailand's economic and employment policy over the past few years. It sketches the events preceding the crisis and the response from the Government and the business sector. It reviews the impact of the crisis on employment and poverty and analyses the measures taken to help employment recover. It also points out some fundamental areas where Thailand's employment policy needs revision and how these deficiencies influenced the development of the crisis itself.

1.1 High growth and the economic crisis

1.1.1 Past performance

(a) Output growth

Before the crisis of 1997, Thailand experienced substantial increases in gross domestic product (GDP) and per capita income. Between 1987 and 1997, the average annual growth rate of the GDP was 8.7 per cent, while for the gross national product (GNP) it was 7.2 per cent per capita. Structural changes had reduced the share of agriculture in the GDP from 23 per cent in 1980 to 11 per cent in 1996 and increased the share of industry from 29 per cent to 40 per cent. The share of services remained relatively unchanged (see Table 1.1).

Table 1.1: Distribution of GDP and employment by sector

Sector	Value-added (per cent of GDP)			Employment by sector (per cent)		
	1980	1990	1996	1980	1990	1996
Agriculture	23	13	11	71	64	50
Industry	29	37	40	10	14	21
Services	48	50	49	19	22	29
Total	100	100	100	100	100	100

Source: World Bank *World Development Indicators 1998* and ILO Key Indicators of the Labour Market database, 1999.

This period produced impressive improvements in life expectancy, infant mortality, child nutrition, adult literacy and primary enrolments. While the fruits of growth were unequally distributed, the benefits trickled down. The result was a decline in the incidence of poverty. In 1997, Thailand ranked relatively high among developing countries on the United Nations Development Programme (UNDP) human poverty index.[1]

---

[1] Thailand was ranked 11th among 78 developing countries. UNDP. 1998. *Human Development Report 1997* (New York, OUP, p. 30).

The main engine of economic growth was manufacturing exports. Thailand's domestic policies included conservative fiscal management, aggressive export promotion and market-oriented interventions. Rural labour moved from traditional agriculture to manufacturing activities and export production. Output of manufactured products grew at an annual rate of 11.3 per cent between 1987 and 1997, while over the same period the value of exports increased by 13.5 per cent per year. High rates of savings and investment also fuelled economic growth. The proportion of foreign investment relative to domestic investment rose. Imported technology and skills contributed to increases in productivity.

Over a 15-year period beginning in 1980, Thailand's rate of growth in the value of both manufactured exports and total exports outranked all of Asia's "high performing economies". This contributed to sustained growth and structural change in the manufacturing sector which moved somewhat up the technological "ladder" from resource-intensive activities towards more complex manufacturing (see Table 1.2).[2]

Table 1.2: Structure of manufacturing production by technological categories, 1970-1994

(Percentages based on current prices)

Technological category	1970	1975	1980	1985	1990	1994
Resource-intensive	54.3	48.8	43.6	46.3	35.1	33.2
Labour-intensive	23.3	28.8	31.2	33.0	34.1	33.6
Scale-intensive	13.8	14.0	16.8	12.1	16.7	14.8
Differentiated	5.0	4.9	5.0	5.1	8.9	12.4
Science-based	3.6	3.5	3.4	3.5	5.2	5.9

Source: The Brooker Group. 1997. BOI Vision Support Doc. (Bangkok), cited in S. Lall. 1998. op. cit., Annex, Table 2, p. 227.

Export-oriented growth during the late 1980s was based on labour-intensive production. During the 1990s, Thailand began to face strong competition from China, Indonesia and Viet Nam with their lower labour costs. One result was a move towards producing more sophisticated goods, e.g. electronic appliances, electrical circuits and vehicle parts. Another has been to look for strategies to reduce costs, such as employing casual labour.

(b) Employment generation

Thailand ratified the ILO Employment Policy Convention, 1964 (No. 122), in 1969, which commits countries to promoting "full, productive and freely chosen" employment. While this ratification was not followed by corresponding legislation or institutional strengthening, Thailand achieved virtual full employment in the early 1990s through fast economic growth based on export-oriented industrialization. High rates of economic growth were accompanied by substantial employment generation. Unemployment rates fell to less than 1 per cent in 1996. Other signs of a tightening labour market included a rise in real wages and an increase in immigrant labour. Thailand became a net receiver of labour resources, with an estimated 1.7 million foreign workers in 1997, most of whom came from Myanmar.

---

[2] S. Lall. 1998. *Thailand's manufacturing competitiveness: An overview*, in NESDB and the World Bank Thailand Office: *Competitiveness and sustainable economic recovery in Thailand*, Vol. 2: Background papers for the Conference on Thailand's Dynamic Economic Recovery and Competitiveness (Bangkok). Resource-intensive refers to natural resources-based activities such as food processing and oil refining.

Both the labour force growth rate and the labour force participation rate have declined since 1990 (see Table 1.3). While the labour force grew at an annual rate of around 3 per cent over the period 1986-1990, the rate declined to 0.4 per cent during 1990-1995. This reflects declining fertility rates and higher rates of school attendance.

Table 1.3: Labour force participation rates, 1990-1998

Year	Total	Male	Female
1990	79.2	84.5	74.0
1994	73.9	80.8	67.2
1998	70.6	78.1	63.2

Source: NSO. *Labour Force Survey*, Round 3, August 1990, 1994 and 1998.

The employment structure became more diverse as more jobs were created in both the modern and informal sectors of urban areas. While agricultural employment as a proportion of the total decreased from three-fifths to one-half over the decade before the crisis, the share of manufacturing employment almost doubled. Employment in construction increased dramatically, and employment in commerce and services also rose. Rapid growth in industry led to rising wage employment. This has been accompanied by a decline in unpaid family work. Over the decade before the crisis, paid employment almost doubled while unpaid work declined from 39 to 30 per cent of total employment. The status in employment of women changed along the same lines as that of men.

During the past two decades, the labour force participation rates of Thai women have been very high, with women slightly under-represented in agriculture, almost equally represented in manufacturing, slightly over-represented in services and under-represented in construction and transport (see Table 1.4). By 1997, the overall percentage of women workers in manufacturing was 65 per cent in six of the leading export industry sectors – food processing (65 per cent); textiles (61 per cent); garments and leather (74 per cent); electronics (75 per cent); gems and jewellery (64 per cent); and plastic and chemicals (45 per cent).[3] Women form a high proportion of the unskilled labour in these industries, but their numbers are few among engineering workers and they are under-represented at the management level as well.

1.1.2 Underlying causes of the crisis

Even before the economic crisis there were signs that Thailand was losing its competitive edge in world markets. Changes in the rates at which productivity increased, as well as costs and exports provided warning signs.

(a) Wages and costs

There was concern among observers that changes in wages, productivity and costs were threatening Thailand's ability to compete with low-wage countries. Table 1.5 shows selected indicators for the manufacturing sector over four periods before the economic crisis. Value-added is measured in constant prices corrected with an index of producer prices relative to

---

[3] ILO/AIT. 1998. *Gender, policy and the economic crisis* (Bangkok, ILO/ROAP, unpublished).

3

Table 1.4: Industrial classification of the employed population, August 1998

Industrial classification	Total		Male (per cent)	Female (per cent)	Females in each industry (per cent)
	Thousands	Per cent			
Agriculture, forestry, hunting and fishing	16,471.5	51.3	52.3	50.0	44.0
Mining and quarrying	41.1	0.1	0.2	0.1	19.7
Manufacturing	4,189.2	13.0	12.1	14.2	49.0
Construction	1,279.5	4.0	6.1	1.4	15.4
Electricity, gas and water	1,770	0.6	0.8	0.2	15.4
Commerce	4,463.4	13.9	11.8	16.5	53.5
Transport, storage and communication	922.6	2.9	4.5	0.9	13.4
Services	4,584.2	14.3	12.2	16.8	53.0
Not adequately defined	7.7	0.0	0.0	0.0	67.5
Total	32,136.2	100.0	100.0	100.0	45.0

Source: NSO. *Labour Force Survey*, Round 3, August 1998.

Table 1.5: Trend rates of growth of selected variables in manufacturing, 1971-1994 – Annual percentage rates

Period	Wages	Value-added	Employment	Productivity	Wage productivity gap
1971-1980	0.16	10.28	6.87	3.41	–3.25
1981-1985	6.05	4.89	5.20	–0.31	1.16
1986-1990	3.91	15.02	7.37	7.65	–3.74
1991-1994	4.53	5.52	4.47	1.05	3.48

Source: World Bank Sources, calculated from Tzannatos. *Growth and inequality in Thailand: An overview of labour market issues*, 5 December 1997, World Bank, mimeo, p. 68.

consumer prices. Productivity is measured as value-added per worker and the wage-productivity gap is the percentage rate of change in wages minus the percentage rate of change in productivity.

The variation over these periods is significant. First, there were considerable increases in output during the 1970s and late 1980s. Slower rates of growth occurred during the early 1980s during structural adjustment. What is of particular interest is the considerable drop in growth rates of manufacturing output during the early 1990s before the economic crisis. Another feature is that rapid growth of manufactured products was accompanied by high rates of productivity growth. Real wage increases appear to be most strongly associated with low output growth. Finally, the "gaps" over these periods show that productivity growth outstripped wage growth during the 1970s and late 1980s. However, during the period of structural adjustment and the years before the economic crisis, wages grew faster than productivity.

Wage increases resulted from changes in domestic labour markets. Rapid growth in industry and services pulled underemployed workers out of agricultural and informal activities. Labour shortages developed as rural labour moved increasingly to the formal sector. As a result, unit labour costs in Thailand have risen far more than those in, for example, Indonesia, China or the Philippines [Tzannatos, 1997].

Thailand may well be losing its competitive position in producing labour-intensive exports based on cheap wage costs. There are calls for a new strategy for export competitiveness. In order to move up the ladder from simple techniques to modern technology, Thailand must find an effective way to implement its strategy to enhance skill development and increase research and technology.

A recent ILO study has reviewed various aspects of wage policy including minimum wages.[4] The findings indicate that the minimum wage has played an important role in influencing increases in real wages and in distributing the fruits of economic growth. With a few exceptions the minimum wage has been adjusted on an annual basis, with changes initially being based on the rate of inflation. The calculation was modified to incorporate changes in economic growth in 1990,[5] and subsequently, minimum wages have increased faster than average wages. Between 1990 and 1996, minimum wages grew by 30 per cent while average wages grew by 23 per cent over the period.[6] Accelerated increases in minimum wages have brought more workers into this pay category, and a large concentration of wage payments around the minimum level has led to wage compression. Minimum wages in relation to the average wage have become relatively high in Thailand. In Bangkok in 1997, the minimum wage was 46 per cent of the average wage. There is some concern that this is producing distorted signals for the allocation of labour and may discourage the provision of training. There is also concern that the setting of minimum wages by a wage committee in the Ministry of Labour and Social Welfare (MOLSW) is replacing wage negotiations through collective bargaining.

The level of minimum wages outside Bangkok has been an additional concern. These are even higher relative to prevailing wages. In 1997, the minimum wage as a percentage of the average wage was 69 per cent in the North. The provincial minimum wage is high by comparison with the average – and by comparison with the minimum wage in Bangkok. The narrow wage differential for unskilled labour between the regions and Bangkok has discouraged investment in the provinces. Recent tripartite discussions with technical input from the ILO and the Asian Development Bank (ADB) have provided advice on the decentralization of minimum wages setting to the National Wage Committee.

(b) Skills and technology

Given Thailand's tight labour market and mid-1990s wage increases outstripping productivity increases, it is critical that education and training meet the demands of a rapidly growing modern sector. This would prepare workers for formal sector jobs, raise productivity in growth industries and prevent increases in real wages from threatening competitiveness.

---

[4] ILO. 1999. *Wage policy and labour competitiveness in Thailand: Summary of main findings of phase one of the study and policy recommendations*, Report prepared for the MOLSW (Bangkok, ILO/EASMAT, unpublished draft).

[5] The formula is the growth rate of the consumer price index plus one-half the growth rate of GDP.

[6] These data are for minimum wages in Bangkok and manufacturing wages in Thailand. They are corrected for price changes using a consumer price index.

As it is difficult to measure skills, other indicators are used as proxy variables. Data are available for formal education and it is clear that Thailand lagged behind its competitors during the years preceding the crisis. A large proportion of the admittedly highly extended labour force has only a primary education. Only half of all children attend secondary school. Relative neglect of secondary education and higher education until recently has resulted in low numbers of skilled workers, acting as a brake on productivity growth. Although government expenditure on education is relatively high, the education system has serious deficiencies, including insufficient emphasis on problem solving, science and maths, inappropriate training in vocational schools, excessive administrative expenditure and insufficient opportunities for teacher training and professional development. World Bank estimates of earnings functions indicate that, other things being equal, the vocational stream of upper secondary education and the technical stream of university education make only a small contribution to earnings differentials.[7]

The current training system is not adequate for improving export competitiveness. Its services are generally limited to meeting enterprises' "operational needs" rather than contributing to upgraded skills or providing new technologies.[8] While reforms were introduced even before the crisis, the effectiveness of proposed changes in policies, institutions and curricula will depend on political commitment.

Although statistics indicate that Thailand is in an intermediate position between high and low technology exports, a closer look at the data shows that the rise in technology-intensive production often only involves minor local contributions and only simple assembly practices required by foreign companies. Thailand has been using a broad range of imported technology rather than developing its own capacity to design and adapt. A number of indicators are a source of concern. Spending on research and development is low. One indicator of the application of technology is the number of International Organization for Standardization (ISO) certificates, and Thailand has relatively few. This suggests that despite its impressive output performance before the economic crisis, Thailand has demonstrated a serious weakness in terms of its technology infrastructure.

(c) Foreign direct investment

Thailand's ability to compete is critically dependent on foreign investment and imported technology. Although domestic firms are fairly strong in terms of labour-intensive activities and resource-based production, foreign companies provide corporate networks, brand names and distribution channels. Yet statistics for foreign direct investment as a percentage of gross fixed capital formation indicate that during the decade before the crisis, Thailand received far less than China and its competitors in Association of South East Asian Nations (ASEAN) countries [Lall, 1999]. In 1995, manufacturing represented a substantial share of foreign direct investment, at 28.8 per cent (see Table 1.6). This share had, however, declined when compared with the average for the years 1970-1994. The same comparison shows that the shares of transport equipment, metal products and construction materials had increased. A breakdown of distribution within manufacturing in 1995 shows that electronic products accounted for the largest portion.

---

[7] Z. Tzannatos. 1997. *Growth and inequality in Thailand: An overview of labour market issues*, Draft 1, p. 45 (Washington D.C., World Bank, unpublished).

[8] S. Lall. 1999. *Raising Competitiveness in the Thai economy*, Paper prepared for the Thailand CEPR (Bangkok, ILO/EASMAT, unpublished).

Table 1.6: Net foreign direct investment by activity

(Billion baht and percentage)

Sector	1970-1974		1995	
	Value	Per cent share	Value	Per cent share
Manufacturing	143.0	36.7	24.3	28.8
Petroleum products	*-9.4*	*-2.4*	*-4.3*	*-8.5*
Chemicals	*23.2*	*6.0*	*2.3*	*4.6*
Electrical and electronic products	*52.2*	*13.4*	*6.0*	*12.0*
Metal and non-metallic products	*17.1*	*4.4*	*2.3*	*4.6*
Machinery and transport equipment	*11.0*	*2.8*	*3.6*	*7.2*
Food	*11.5*	*3.0*	*1.2*	*2.5*
Construction materials	*0.9*	*0.2*	*0.6*	*1.3*
Textiles and garments	*10.9*	*2.8*	*1.0*	*1.9*
Others	*25.7*	*6.6*	*1.7*	*3.3*
Trade and services	76.9	19.7	11.5	23.1
Construction	43.1	11.1	0.9	1.8
Financial institutions	30.8	7.9	0.6	1.3
Mining and quarrying	22.0	5.7	1.3	2.5
Agriculture	3.2	0.8	...	...
Others	70.6	18.1	21.1	42.5
Total	389.7	100.0	49.7	100.0

Source: Bank of Thailand data cited in S. Lall. 1998. *Thailand's manufacturing competitiveness*, op cit.

The Thai Board of Investment's *Foreign Investors Confidence Survey* of May 1997 looked at factors that were considered to play the most important role in attracting foreign direct investment to Thailand. Three-quarters of the respondents identified "labour costs". This suggests that Thailand is not attracting investors who use advanced technology and require an educated workforce, but is still attempting to compete with low-wage economies for labour-intensive production. There were large falls in low-technology exports between 1995 and 1998 and resource-based exports decreased steadily over the same period. However, some apparently technology-intensive products also benefit from the low wage costs of semi-skilled labour when their local operations involve simple assembly. Thus, rising wage costs may explain the relatively weak export performance of technology-intensive products before the crisis.

(d) Infrastructure bottlenecks and transaction costs

Other structural problems for Thai export competitiveness are infrastructure bottlenecks and transaction costs. High growth rates strained Thailand's capacity to provide transport, telecommunications, power and water. Its ability to attract foreign investors and promote export competitiveness has been threatened by high transaction costs in the form of rules, regulations, corruption and inefficiency. Lall writes that the May 1997 Thai Board of Investment survey shows that red tape, customs administration and official corruption are among the biggest obstacles to the success of Thai exports.[9]

---

[9] Cited in S. Lall. 1999. *Raising competitiveness*, op. cit., p. 35. More specifically, transaction costs are associated with *business entry* (registration, licensing, property rights, rules, clarity, predictability, enforcement and conflict resolution), *business exit* (bankruptcy, liquidation, severance/layoffs, rules, clarity, predictability, enforcement and conflict resolution) and *business operation* (taxation, trade-related regulation, labour hiring/firing, contracting, logistics, rules, clarity, predictability, enforcement and conflict resolution).

(e) Environmental degradation

Rapid economic growth has brought substantial environmental degradation. Rural-urban migration has led to unregulated land development that places enormous pressure on infrastructure and services and highlights inadequacies in the legal, institutional and supervisory framework for land use management. Air and water pollution has increased production costs and affects both quality and competitiveness. Air pollution and traffic congestion have discouraged foreign investment. Water pollution has affected seafood exports.[10] Failure to meet environmental standards may well jeopardize international competitiveness.

1.1.3 Trigger factors

Some of the immediate causes of the economic crisis are associated with apparent success. Rapid economic growth, conservative macro-economic policies and a pegged exchange rate attracted an increasing amount of foreign investment. Most of the foreign capital inflows took the form of short-term borrowing, especially after the creation of the Bangkok International Banking Facility in 1993. A slow down in external demand pushed down the value of exports in 1996 – at the same time that rising costs and prices caused internal supply shocks (see Table 1.7).

Table 1.7: Key economic indicators, 1994-1998

	1995	1996	1997	1998
Real GDP growth (average annual per cent)	8.8	5.5	–0.4	–9.4
Consumer price inflation (average annual per cent)	5.8	5.9	5.7	8.1
Merchandise exports fob (millions of dollars)	55,447	54,408	56,652	52,873
Merchandise imports fob (millions of dollars)	63,415	63,897	55,100	36,946*
Debt-service ratio paid (per cent)	11.1	1.6	14.8	19.3*
Exchange rate (average baht: dollar)	24.92	25.34	31.36	41.36

Source: Economist Intelligence Unit, Thailand, 3rd quarter 1999.
      * Estimates.

In July 1997, the Bank of Thailand abandoned its currency peg and introduced a managed float. The subsequent devaluation sharply increased the baht cost of servicing foreign debt. Loss of investor confidence cut sources of foreign borrowing. Net private capital inflows were replaced by massive capital outflows. Diminishing foreign reserves led the Thai Government to seek help from the International Monetary Fund (IMF) in August 1997.

---

[10] Over-fishing also threatens to deplete marine resources. In 1993 Thailand became the world's largest exporter of fishery products.

8

1.1.4 Macro-economic reforms and weaknesses

Much has been written about the economic causes of the economic crisis. There were structural weaknesses during the boom period. The financial system suffered from inadequate accounting practices, prudential supervision, disclosure rules and bankruptcy laws. Close ties between banks and clients replaced project evaluation, financial analysis and risk management. Financial liberalization facilitated by the opening of the Bangkok International Banking Facility was not accompanied by appropriate mechanisms for monitoring and evaluation. Restrictive monetary policy and a pegged exchange rate encouraged massive capital inflows and produced distorted investment decisions. The corporate sector, dominated by family enterprises, lacked transparency and accountability.

Thailand's savings rate was high, but its investment rate was even higher. The difference was accommodated by a large deficit on current account of the balance of payments. Foreign direct investment as a proportion of inflows fell substantially in the decade before the crisis. The private sector mainly financed higher investment by borrowing abroad on short maturities. The growth of portfolio capital relative to foreign exchange reserves left Thailand vulnerable to the speculation that followed a reduction of exports. This was made possible by the removal of capital controls and the gap between foreign and domestic rates of interest. Structural weaknesses in financial institutions and the corporate sector directed foreign capital to purchases of real estate rather than productive investment. Further, both the financial and corporate sectors suffered from outdated laws and regulations determining property rights and corporate relations.

1.1.5 Crisis impact on labour markets

The economic recession has led to a drop in employment and increases in unemployment and underemployment. This has resulted in substantial reductions in wages and earnings. These changes are all the more significant when measured against the level of economic activity that might have been recorded had growth trends continued.

(a) Employment, unemployment and underemployment

Data from the Labour Force Survey of February 1999 show a total of 32.8 million persons in the labour force (see Table 1.8).[11] Of these, 30.0 million were employed and 1.7 million unemployed. An additional 1.1 million were seasonally inactive. Favourable employment trends up to 1996 or so were reversed in the period following the crisis. Employment fell from 30.3 million in February 1997 to 29.4 million in February 1998. By the first quarter of 1999 it had not returned to its 1997 level. Between 1997 and 1999, the number of unemployed more than doubled from some 700,000 to 1.7 million and the unemployment rate increased from 2.2 per cent to 5.2 per cent.[12] Time-related underemployment has also increased significantly in the period since the crisis [Kakwani, 1998].

Employment: According to National Economic and Social Development Board (NESDB) calculations, employment growth for women has been less than that for men with annual growth

---

[11] Data from the first quarter or round 1 are used as these are the most recent figures. However it should be noted that this is the dry season when seasonal unemployment is greatest.

[12] This is based on the "relaxed definition of unemployment" that includes those who are available for work but not actually seeking work.

Table 1.8: Labour force status, February 1994-1999

(Thousands)

	1994	1995	1996	1997	1998	1999
Total population	59,034.9	59,112.9	59,750.4	60,350.7	60,949.0	61,551.2
Total labour force	31,049.9	31,347.9	31,898.4	32,000.2	32,143.1	32,810.2
Employed	28,233.5	29,055.1	30,099.2	30,266.4	29,412.9	30,024.5
Unemployed	1,244.3	723.5	641.3	697.9	1,479.3	1,715.6
– *Looking for work*	*200.1*	*167.8*	*119.6*	*179.6*	*402.8*	*475.8*
– *Available but not actively seeking work*	*1,044.2*	*555.7*	*521.7*	*518.3*	*1,076.5*	*1,239.8*
Seasonally inactive	1,571.9	1,569.2	1,157.8	1,035.9	1,250.8	1,069.8
Unemployment rate (per cent)	4.0	2.3	2.0	2.2	4.6	5.2

Source: NSO. *Labour Force Survey*, Round 1, February, various years.

rates before the crisis of 0.4 per cent and 1.0 per cent respectively. Female employment is more likely to be affected by seasonal fluctuations than male employment. But in terms of the crisis it appears that the reduction in employment has been slightly smaller for women than for men. The "crisis" index calculated by the National Economic and Social Development Board showing divergence from a "trend" indicates that for the first quarter of 1998 employment was down by 2.1 per cent (1.4 per cent for women and 2.7 per cent for men).[13]

Data in Table 1.9, collected in February of each year, are not corrected for trends. They show that between 1997 and 1999 the number of private employees declined by 12.2 per cent while government employees increased by 9.1 per cent. The table also shows a shift from paid employment to self-employment with considerable increases for employers (22.1 per cent) and own-account workers (8.5 per cent).

Table 1.9: Employment by status, February 1996-1999

(Millions)

	1996	1997	1998	1999
Employers	0.84	0.77	0.78	0.94
Government employees	2.31	2.42	2.67	2.64
Private employees	11.68	11.64	10.68	10.22
Own-account workers	9.37	9.30	9.48	10.09
Unpaid family workers	5.90	6.14	5.80	6.13
Total	30.10	30.27	29.41	30.02

Source: NSO. *Labour Force Survey*, Round 1, February 1996-1999.

---

[13] NESDB. 1998. *Indicators of well-being and policy analysis: The Impact of economic crisis on standards of living in Thailand*, in *NESDB Newsletter*, Vol. 2, No. 4, p. 6, Oct. 1998. This paper has fitted a non-linear model to data obtained from the Labour Force Survey for the period 1992-1998. The model controls for "seasonality" in data for the wet season (first quarter) and dry season (third quarter) of each year as well as "trends" over the seven-year period. By controlling for both seasons and trends, the model is able to indicate changes in the utilization of labour and income per worker that may be associated with the economic downturn. Thus, the crisis indices indicate the deviation between actual events from what might have been had the trend continued.

Unemployment: Measured unemployment in Thailand is usually relatively low. If only those actively seeking work are counted as unemployed it is usually under one per cent. The Labour Force Survey uses a definition that closely approximates the international standard, so that those classified as unemployed must have worked for less than one hour during the reference week. Thus, casual workers on daily contracts are not included in the unemployed population, although they may be unemployed for most of the week. If the "relaxed" definition of unemployment is used, including those available for work but not actively looking for a job, the unemployment rate was significantly higher in February 1999 than the figure produced by the strict definition of active job search (5.2 per cent compared to 1.5 per cent). It should also be remembered that laid-off workers do not necessarily appear in active unemployment figures. Many go directly into other jobs (sometimes in the informal sector) or leave the labour force (described as discouraged workers).

The unemployment rate among women is higher than among men. In February 1999, the corresponding figures were 5.8 per cent and 5.1 per cent respectively. However, the gap has been narrowing. National Economic and Social Development Board indicators show that the crisis had a greater impact on unemployment rates for men than for women. The crisis indices for unemployment rates by age groups indicate that workers in the age range of 30-50 years were most affected. Figures for the third quarter of 1998 indicate that unemployment among people in their 30s and 40s rose by about 80 per cent.

Underemployment: The underemployment of a large number of industrial workers that has occurred in the wake of the crisis is a new phenomenon. Many employers chose to cut working hours in order to avoid severance pay obligations. Time-related underemployment measured in terms of persons working fewer than 35 hours per week was declining before the crisis but increased sharply in its wake. Between February 1997 and 1998 the number of people working fewer than 35 hours per week increased by almost 2 million, from 2.43 million (7.6 per cent of the labour force) to 4.41 million (13.7 per cent of the labour force). The greatest numbers of underemployed workers in 1998 were in agriculture, manufacturing and commerce. The largest increase was in manufacturing. The increase was more significant in urban areas than rural areas. Among those underemployed in urban areas almost half of the men and three-quarters of the women were in the industrial sector.

Alternative methods which could be used to measure labour slack would include underemployment in terms of earnings per worker or mismatches of skills. Data from various sources indicate that many workers are receiving lower than expected earnings and new graduates are finding only casual work.

(b) Layoffs

Official statistics show that the reported number of terminated employees increased from 5,015 in 1996 to 41,927 in 1997 and 51,960 in 1998. Data show that 53 per cent of laid-off workers in 1998 were women. Naturally the percentages of retrenched women workers were especially high in some sectors: garments (95 per cent), toys (88 per cent), knitting (80 per cent), electrical appliances and electrical goods (80 per cent), jewellery (73 per cent), department stores (73 per cent), plastic products (71 per cent) and shoes and leather goods (68 per cent).[14] Layoffs in these sectors occurred because, despite the devaluation of the baht, the value

---

[14] N. Theeravit. 1999. *Towards gender equality at work in Thailand*, Report prepared for ILO/EASMAT (Bangkok, unpublished).

of exports fell in the first six months of 1998 for labour-intensive products. Given that these products are often produced through a putting-out system, a large number of women working in the informal sector may also have lost employment and income.

Of the 1.3 million persons who were reported as "former workers" in the February 1998 Labour Force Survey, two-fifths (39.6 per cent) had been employed in construction and another 29.9 per cent had been working in manufacturing.

(c) Wages and earnings

Evidence of the drop in wages during the crisis comes from a number of sources.

Kakwani and Pothong (1998) use data from the labour force surveys covering all sectors of the economy to calculate a measure for the standard of living.[15] Their data show a decline of 11.5 per cent between the third quarter of 1997 and the first quarter of 1998. The reduction in the subsequent period was 2.4 per cent. If a crisis index is used to control for long-term trends, the drop in per capita income was 19.2 per cent rather than 11.5 per cent for the first quarter of 1998. This means that the standard of living was four-fifths of what it would have been if growth had continued.

Data from the Labour Force Survey for the period covering February 1997 to February 1998 indicate that nominal wages declined by 6 per cent on average for all workers. The fall in real wages was greater in urban (8.3 per cent) than in rural areas (4.7 per cent). For the country as a whole, the decrease was about the same for males and females. However, in urban areas the decline in real wages was greater for women than for men. The reverse is true for rural areas. Thus, male-female disparities rose in urban areas and fell in rural areas.

In urban areas the nominal wages of women workers declined by 1.6 per cent, implying a 10.5 per cent decline in real wages. The decrease in real wages was especially severe in manufacturing, where the decline was 4 per cent in nominal terms and 13 per cent in real terms. For men, construction wages in urban areas fell 15 per cent in nominal terms and 24 per cent in real terms. The National Economic and Social Development Board shows that by the first quarter of 1999, the economic downturn had reduced the real monthly income of wage earners by 10.5 per cent from the level expected with continued growth.

According to data for the formal sector obtained through establishment surveys, nominal wages increased by 3.8 per cent between 1997 and 1998, giving a fall in real terms of 4.0 per cent. This fall was greater for the largest enterprises employing at least 100 workers (-4.5 per cent) than for the smallest enterprises with one to four employees (-2.7 per cent). Not surprisingly, average real wages of those earning a daily wage dropped more than those for monthly workers and salaried employees.[16]

---

[15] NESDB. op. cit. This measure takes into account incomes of all persons who are employed, unemployed, seasonally unemployed and those who are not in the labour force. It is deflated by using "spatial price indices" calculated by Kakwani. Per capita income is then computed by multiplying the average real income of each region by the number of earners in the region and dividing by the regional population. In order to correct for "seasonal" fluctuations and secular "trends" a non-linear model is used to derive indices that show the separate effects of seasons, trends and the crisis.

[16] MOLSW. 1998. *Yearbook of Labour Statistics, 1998* (Bangkok, Department of Labour Protection and Welfare). Data are deflated by the consumer price indices from the Department of Business Economics (Ministry of Commerce).

(d) Internal migration

It was generally assumed at the onset of the crisis that an increase in urban unemployment would lead to urban-rural migration. Rossarin Gray points out that the massive gross flows between urban and rural areas that had been common for some time continued at similar levels during the economic crisis, noting: "What was different in 1998 was the decreased capacity of rural areas to absorb normal migration flows". The highest unemployment rates were for urban-to-rural migrants who were surveyed in rural areas during August 1998. Among those in the labour force almost one-eighth were unemployed.[17]

There is obviously a close link between unemployment and migration. Migrants have different labour force participation and unemployment rates from non-migrants. Recent migrants are likely to have relatively low labour force participation rates and relatively high unemployment rates. For those who have moved within the last year, high rates of unemployment are notable for men in urban areas and women in rural areas.[18]

Labour Force Survey data for the first quarter of 1998 indicate that 4.7 million people of 13 years of age and over had lived in their current place of residence for less than one year. Unemployment rates for these recent migrants were generally higher than for non-migrants and for those who moved more than one year before the survey.

(e) International labour migration and trafficking of women and children

Thailand has passed through a full migration cycle moving from serving as a major source of labour to the Middle East and Asia to becoming a major destination for migrant workers from neighbouring low-income countries. Before entering a period of rapid economic growth, Thailand relied on sending contract labour to provide a safety valve for domestic unemployment and a valuable source of foreign exchange. During the 1990s, Asian countries replaced the Middle East as the major destination.

This shift has led to problems, especially in terms of the protection of migrant workers. Many unskilled workers have to migrate as undocumented migrants in the absence of a regular policy to admit such workers on the part of major labour-shortage countries. At the same time, female migration has increased rapidly. Undocumented migration for the entertainment and sex trades means that the actual share of female migration may be much higher than official statistics show. This migration often occurs through organized trafficking. Whether trafficked or not, these workers are extremely vulnerable.

With an estimated 450,000 Thai workers abroad, the protection of overseas workers has become a major issue for Thai policy makers. The crisis has led to increased emigration pressures with the Government actively encouraging out-migration. Yet authorities have found it difficult to control various abuses by recruitment agents in the form of fraud and high fees.

The presence since the early 1990s of a large number of unskilled and mostly undocumented foreign migrant workers provides a further problem. The Ministry of Labour and Social Welfare believes that there are close to one million undocumented workers. Thailand's

---

[17] Rossarin Gray. 1999. *The effects of globalization on labour force and migration in Thailand*, Paper prepared for the Asia and Pacific Policy Seminar on the Impact of Globalization on Population Change and Poverty in Rural Areas (Bangkok, UN-ESCAP).

[18] *Ibid.*, p. ii.

concern about irregular migration was clearly demonstrated when the Thai Government convened the International Symposium towards Regional Cooperation on Irregular Undocumented Migration (21-23 April 1999). This Symposium was a major initiative, and produced a significant statement in the form of the Bangkok Declaration.[19]

Within Thailand, most undocumented workers come from Myanmar. Generally, these workers are employed in "3D jobs" – dirty, dangerous and demanding occupations normally shunned by local workers – at one-half to one-third the wages that local workers will accept. In past years, Thai employers, especially those in border provinces, have consistently lobbied the Government to preserve access to this cheap source of labour and have managed to secure the introduction of a work permit scheme. The economic crisis has caused a sharp reversal of this policy. Immigrant worker replacement is a major component in the unemployment relief programme, although pressure from employers has led to exemptions in particular sectors, including fishery. Government estimates indicate that about 250,000 undocumented workers have already left or have been repatriated. However, long borders together with enforcement problems have made repatriation difficult. Given poor working conditions and low wages, local workers are simply not willing to accept some of the arduous work and hazardous jobs performed by foreign workers.

Thailand has also become a major hub for the trafficking of women and children for commercial sex and other exploitative purposes from neighbouring countries by organized criminal groups. The relatively low status accorded to women and girls in society and the lack of information and education among rural and tribal communities and their abject poverty make girls easy targets for sexual exploitation. Women and children of ethnic minorities and tribal groups, and those who were trafficked from abroad and illegally reside in Thailand, are at particularly high risk. Unfortunately, the common practice has been to punish the victims rather than the perpetrators. The Bangkok Declaration recognized this problem and made the following recommendation: "The participating countries and region should be encouraged to pass legislation to criminalize smuggling of and trafficking in human beings, especially women and children, in all its forms and purposes, including as sources of cheap labour, and to cooperate as necessary in the prosecution and penalisation of all offenders, especially international organised criminal groups".

NGOs have been in the forefront of the struggle against commercial sexual exploitation and the trafficking of children and women. Since the early 1990s, the Ministry of Labour and Social Welfare, the Ministry of Education and several provincial governments have joined this effort. Within the Ministry of Labour and Social Welfare, the Department of Public Welfare is one of the key agencies involved with the implementation of the National Policy and Plan of Action for the Prevention and Eradication of the Commercial Sexual Exploitation of Children, which has been developed under the aegis of the National Commission on Women's Affairs. This includes a number of initiatives relating to vocational training and business start-up incentives; awareness-raising and education for vulnerable girls and women; a hotline to combat child exploitation and child prostitution; and shelter, vocational training and counselling services for ex-commercial sex workers and other children and women who have been subject to abuse. Major subregional programmes to combat the trafficking of women and children in the greater Mekong subregion will become operational in the near future with ILO assistance. Successful

---

[19] The Bangkok Declaration on Irregular Migration, adopted by the International Symposium on Towards Regional Cooperation on Irregular Undocumented Migration (21-23 April 1999, Bangkok).

strategies, developed in Thailand, will be replicated and expanded to reduce both internal and cross-border trafficking for labour exploitation in the subregion.

(f)   Vulnerable groups

Vulnerable groups have been hit harder by the economic crisis than other persons. Among those identified are street children, the elderly poor, young people, sex workers, HIV/AIDS sufferers, disabled persons, migrant workers, ethnic minorities and religious minorities.

Children: The Labour Force Survey does not collect data on any economic activity for children under 13.[20] Using information for the 13-24 and 15-19 year age brackets, the number of working children in Thailand fell sharply as economic growth increased during the 1990s. Between 1991 and 1997, labour force participation rates for children aged 13-14 years in the "off season" for agriculture declined from 29.1 per cent to 8.6 per cent. The corresponding figures for the "peak season" in agriculture are higher. In 1997, one-tenth of the children in this age group were economically active. Participation rates for teenagers decreased from 65.0 per cent during the 1991 dry season to 35.3 per cent in 1997. In 1997, 39.0 per cent were economically active during the wet season.

The decline in labour force participation rates can be attributed to both poverty reduction and increased education. The proportion of children aged 13-14 years attending school increased from 61.5 per cent in 1991 to 87.6 per cent in 1997. The corresponding figures for the 15-19 year age group rose from 27.7 per cent to 57.5 per cent. By 1997, more girls (88.9 per cent) than boys (86.4 per cent) in the 13-14 age group were in school. The same held true for the 15-19 year age group, with 58.4 per cent of the girls and 56.6 per cent of the boys in school.

Despite fears to the contrary, children's labour force participation rates do not appear to have increased with the crisis. In February 1999, the activity rates for the 13-14 year age group remained about the same (8.5 per cent), while those for teenagers 15-19 years of age continued to decline (32.7 per cent). Activity rates are lower for girls than for boys and for urban areas than for rural areas.

Thailand permits the employment of children between the ages of 15 and 18 years under certain conditions. Regulations prohibit children from working in environments that are hazardous to their health and govern the location of employment for children. Certain jobs have minimum age requirements. However, anecdotal evidence suggests that the economic crisis has resulted in an increase in child labour in prohibited environments. It has also increased the likelihood of employment as agricultural workers, street vendors and domestic servants.[21]

Youth: Youth can be defined as those aged 15-24 years. The most recent data from the Labour Force Survey for the first quarter of 1999 show a total of 6.1 million youth in the labour force. Of these 5,014,200 are employed, 720,800 are unemployed and 322,800 are seasonally inactive. Among economically active youth, 43.5 per cent are young women.

---

[20] The ILO has recommended that labour force statistics be collected for the population aged ten years and above.

[21] UNDP. 1999. *Common Country Assessment for Thailand* (Bangkok, UN Resident Coordinator System, UNDP).

Youth labour force participation rates are 52.8 per cent, with 58.7 per cent for young men and 46.7 per cent for young women. The unemployment rate for youth (11.9 per cent) is three times higher than that for adults (3.7 per cent). The unemployment rate for teenagers (14.3 per cent) is higher than that for young adults (10.8 per cent). The figure for young men (13.2 per cent) is higher than that for young women (10.2 per cent). Youth unemployment rates are higher in rural areas (12.5 per cent) than in urban areas (9.2 per cent).

Although unemployment rates are higher for young people than for the adult population, the impact of the crisis has not been as severe for youth as for adults. National Economic and Social Development Board data show that for the third quarter of 1998 the unemployment rates for the population aged 16-18 years and 19-24 years were 32 per cent and 37 per cent respectively. Although these rates were higher than the levels projected if growth had continued, by the first quarter of 1999 the unemployment rates for young people did not deviate substantially from the long-term trend.

People with disabilities: Problems of dependence and poverty among disabled persons were common in Thailand before the crisis. Inadequate information makes it difficult to determine the impact of the economic downturn on the employment of disabled persons. For those who had protection the crisis may have made little difference. For others, it may have increased the possibility of being laid off and reduced opportunities for new job seekers. For those who were self-employed, the crisis can be expected to have reduced demand for their goods and services with a subsequent fall in income and rising risk of bankruptcy. It is feared that reductions in Government expenditure may have adversely affected benefits such as public services, income support and training. A decline in official support and private donations has also forced many NGOs to cut back on support for vulnerable groups. According to Murray: "For disabled people reliant on charity, who are already barely managing to survive, the economic downturn may hit hardest of all, as their benefactors felt the economic pinch".[22]

Nevertheless, there are some positive developments. The Ministry of Education has recently conducted a campaign on the theme of equitable access to educational resources. Thailand's new 1997 Constitution establishes an enabling environment for disabled persons by offering protection against discriminatory practices and guaranteeing rights to basic education for not less than 12 years. Other notable changes include increasing employment opportunities in public services and state enterprises; cash assistance for the severely disabled provided by the Department of Public Welfare; and tax breaks for those caring for people with disabilities.

1.1.6 Social impact of the economic crisis

(a) Poverty and inequality

Despite Thailand's remarkable success in terms of economic growth and employment generation before the crisis, it was acknowledged that income and wealth disparities were widening across individuals, regions and sectors. The Eighth National Economic and Social Development Plan placed an emphasis on the reduction of disparities and people-centred development.

The crisis had an obvious impact on poverty. As the crisis developed, poverty rose significantly. According to the National Economic and Social Development Board, the

---

[22] Barbara Murray. 1998. *Vocational training of disabled persons in Thailand: A challenge to policy-makers* (Bangkok, ILO/EASMAT).

incidence of poverty increased after decades of decline. The numbers of poor rose from 6.8 million in 1996 to 7.9 million in 1998 and the percentage below the poverty line from 11.3 per cent to 12.7 per cent, reversing a long trend in poverty reduction.

There have been significant differences in the development of poverty by region. The largest increases were in the Northeast and South. Poverty has increased less in rural areas (from 19.3 per cent in 1996 to 22.7 per cent in 1998) than in urban areas (from 11.4 per cent in 1996 to 15.6 per cent in 1998).

(b) Education, health and nutrition

Dropout rates from schools and universities appear to have been increasing before the economic crisis but accelerated as it struck. Especially vulnerable are poor households living near the poverty line. "Family problems" – both financial and social – were seen as the principal explanation of dropouts. Although efforts were made to protect education budgets, there appear to have been cutbacks in expenditure. An Asian Development Bank study shows that two-fifths of schools surveyed reported cuts averaging 27 per cent.[23] Nominal budgets have been eroded by the increased costs of school supplies, and supplementary income from non-governmental sources (families and communities) has dropped. In addition, Budgetary disbursements have not been timely and reliable. This is particularly true of funding for school lunches and teaching materials. A United Nations Children's Fund (UNICEF) study found that debt has forced some teachers to engage in moonlighting activities.[24] All these develop-ments have weakened the quality of education.

A rise in the use of public health facilities has been accompanied by a fall in the use of private medical care. Prices of pharmaceuticals rose with the depreciation of the baht. The Health Systems Research Institute reported that by November 1997 the price of domestically produced drugs had risen by 12 to 15 per cent, while the cost of imported drugs had gone up by 18 to 20 per cent.[25] The increased use of public health facilities may also reflect the success of Thailand's health card scheme. Overall, it appears that people are coping with the crisis by switching to public facilities, postponing medical attention and resorting to self-medication. There are also alarming signs of reduced care. According to a study whose findings were reported in the *Bangkok Post*, most jobless pregnant women from lower income groups had to pay for their own medical expenses despite a government support policy. Twenty per cent of such women who had lost their jobs paid all their own expenses, while 53 per cent had to buy health cards under the government scheme. The same study also reported that more underweight children were born to unemployed women with lower incomes.[26] In addition to basic health care the crisis has affected stress-related ailments.

---

[23] The Brooker Group Consortium. 1999. *Synthesis of findings and policy implications* pp. 14-15 (Bangkok, 31 May 1999).

[24] Mehotra, Santosh: *Mitigating the social impact of the economic crisis: A review of the Royal Thai Government's response*, Paper prepared for UNICEF (New York, 1998).

[25] Cited in World Bank. 1999. *Thailand Social Monitor, Challenge for social reform*, p. 11 (Bangkok, World Bank Thailand Office).

[26] A. Bhatiasevi: "Health care scheme fails to help poor pregnant women", in *Bangkok Post*, (Bangkok, 31 Aug. 1999).

1.2 Current policies

1.2.1 Measures toward recovery

Following the collapse of the baht, the Ministry of Finance and the Bank of Thailand worked in conjunction with the IMF to implement an austerity programme. Tight monetary policy and reduced government expenditure were combined with financial system reform. These policies failed to stabilize markets and restore confidence; they also further depressed domestic demand and deepened the economic recession. Companies and banks faced with high debt burdens were close to bankruptcy, while the baht and stock prices continued to plummet.

The austerity package was criticized for several reasons. Some pointed to the high social costs of bankruptcies among otherwise viable enterprises. Others argued that the government was "coerced" into introducing structural reforms as part of stabilization packages at a time of political fragility. Critics suggest ulterior motives for liberalizing laws relating to foreign ownership, saying such changes allow private businesses to be purchased at distress prices and clear the way for the sale of state enterprises to foreign companies. However, it is always difficult to assess what the situation would have been under different circumstances.

Austerity policies gave way to reflation. An economic stimulus package was introduced in March 1999 with expansionary fiscal policies and reduced energy prices, as well as government expenditure to increase employment and generate income. The package included special measures to address the social ills faced by underprivileged groups and those seriously affected by the economic crisis.

Other measures are underway to recapitalize the financial sector and restructure non-performing loans. A Financial Sector Restructuring Agency was created to auction assets (mostly non-performing loans) held by the Government. A Corporate Debt Restructuring Advisory Committee was established to facilitate restructuring of debt in the corporate sector. A legal framework is being established to allow creditors a mechanism to pursue bankruptcy and foreclosure.

A major reform of the tariff system is now under way in order to reduce input costs for exporters. This reform also forms part of a commitment to liberalize services in conformity with World Trade Organization guidelines. Reforms include reduced tariffs on capital goods, raw materials and other products and removal of the import duty surcharge. Although privatization does form part of the policy package, this has been delayed, due in part to objections from public sector workers who fear widespread job losses. Output data for the third quarter of 1999[27] suggests that it is unlikely that the stimulus package for job creation will produce sustainable results quickly. Growing consumer confidence has not been translated into rising private investment. Investment continued to contract, albeit at a slower rate than in 1998. Despite lower rates of interest and a more stable baht, there was inadequate expansion of credit and considerable over-capacity in industry.

By August 1999, the Government was nonetheless confident that domestic economic stability and exchange rate stability had been achieved.

---

[27] EIU. 1999. *Country report, Thailand, 3rd quarter* (London).

(a) Action plan for unemployment relief

A number of measures were introduced to address the hardships caused by the crisis. The Government introduced a seven-point unemployment relief plan in November 1997. The plan was designed to create rural employment opportunities; encourage industrial sector employment; curb the use of immigrant labour; promote overseas employment; boost living standards through open markets, cheap commodities and business loans; promote a new agricultural model; and reduce business costs of social security (see Chapter 2, Section 2.2).

(b) Special projects for disadvantaged groups

Several projects have been targeted toward disadvantaged groups. Some were initiated through the Social Sector Programme Loan of the Asian Development Bank. Before October 1998, the Cabinet approved projects focusing on a scholarship fund and voluntary health cards. By December 1998, several more had been approved dealing with computer training, labour market information, employment-creation projects, pre-school support; lunch and milk for disadvantaged children; and a community unemployment register. Another project aims to build leadership and networks among home workers. A Japan International Cooperation Agency project is intended to enhance the capacity of leaders of home workers through training courses. Under the Social Investment Programme of the World Bank, a regional vocational training programme was established to assist retrenched workers, women workers and child labour. An Overseas Economic Cooperation Fund loan project under the programme was designed to promote eco-tourism in highland areas. The Social Security Fund is being used to supply low-interest loans under special conditions through four commercial banks.

(c) Action plan for improved competitiveness of the labour force

The action plan prepared by the Ministry of Labour and Social Welfare in February 1999 includes five major components:[28]

(i)   Changes in labour legislation and labour regulations to eliminate duplication and ambiguity in three major acts (the Labour Protection Act 1975, the Social Security Act, 1990 and the Workmen's Compensation Act) and other related regulations;

(ii)   Better wage policies;

(iii) Expanding the Employee Assistance Scheme covering social security and labour protection for both the informal and formal sectors. A high-level task force is to consider safety nets in an integrated fashion (including severance pay, a worker welfare fund and unemployment insurance);

(iv)   Promotion of better labour relations among employers and workers;

(v)   Raising the skill levels of the workforce drawing on the existing Human Resource Development Master Plan.

(d) Overview

It is too early to assess the impact of policies developed and implemented in response to the crisis. However, anecdotal evidence suggests that some leakages may have occurred through inefficiency and corruption, and that projects have not been targeted directly enough to achieve

---

[28] MOLSW. 1999. *Action plan to improve competitiveness of the labour force*, (internal doc.).

employment objectives.[29]   Some employment schemes have only provided employment of limited duration for those seeking work and those who benefited were not always retrenched workers and the unemployed. It may be that temporary projects merely replaced resources from ongoing programmes. Elsewhere staff resources needed to maintain basic services were diverted to emergency projects. While donor agencies have provided monitoring and evaluation support, a stronger national labour market information system would have enabled policy makers to form a clearer picture of the usefulness of these responses to the crisis.

1.2.2 Promoting gender equality

Thailand's first policies specifically aimed at helping working women appeared in the early 1970s. These focused primarily on rural women and were geared toward strengthening their roles as mothers and housewives. The first long-term women's development plan (1982-2001) stressed women's involvement in poverty alleviation programmes through income generation and training opportunities. In the early 1990s, policies emphasized women's contribution to national development and their equal involvement in that process. The second long-term plan for women (1992-2011) emphasises equality between women and men. It aims to eliminate all discrimination against women, especially working women and disadvantaged groups. Thailand's 1997 Constitution reaffirmed the equal rights of women and men.

Since the mid-1990s, several laws have been developed or revised which have a special bearing on women workers. The Prostitution Prevention and Suppression Act, 1996 and the Act on the Traffic of Women and Children, 1997 (amended) aim at decriminalizing and protecting the victims and impose harsher penalties on the clients and organizers of the sex trade. The Labour Protection Act, 1998 reiterates the importance of equal treatment of women and men in employment. It has extended maternity protection by explicitly prohibiting the dismissal of women on the grounds of pregnancy and for the first time legally recognizes sexual harassment at the workplace as a crime. The Government has also acknowledged the need to improve protection for home-based workers, 95 per cent of whom are women. The new Labour Protection Act officially covers home workers but will be applied only after rules have been issued for its implementation.

1.2.3 Social protection and safety net measures

Before the crisis, Thailand had not developed a comprehensive system for social protection and public assistance. There are several possible explanations for this. First, the many years of rapid growth made the need for special anti-poverty programmes and social safety nets seem less urgent. Second, Thai society has placed a high value on self-reliance and family responsibility. Finally, many felt that such programmes would place an unnecessary burden on public expenditure and government administration.

The ILO's 1998 report, The Social Impact of the Asian Economic Crisis, stated: "One of the clearest lessons to emerge from the crisis is that the existing systems of social protection were unable to cope adequately with its social consequences".

Much of the debate that has accompanied the crisis has concerned the extent to which the Government should improve formal social security schemes as opposed to encouraging less official mechanisms. Revisions to the Eighth National Economic and Social Development Plan were intended to respond to the gaps in protection by (i) minimizing the effects of

---

[29] See Chapter 2, Section 2.2 for details.

rising unemployment through measures to alleviate unemployment in urban areas and promote employment generation in the rural areas to absorb returning migrants; (ii) assisting underprivileged groups of people and those affected by the crisis through social welfare, education and health; and (iii) preventing and alleviating social problems, especially drug use and crimes as well as promoting commendable social values.

A number of programmes have been launched to support job creation, income maintenance, social security and community initiatives. Debate continues over the extent of government programmes for unemployment insurance and the role of informal mechanisms of self-reliance and self-help. What is clear is that existing systems need to be adjusted.

National Statistical Office (NSO) figures indicate that severance pay has not cushioned many workers against income loss. The Labour Force Survey for February 1998 revealed that of those who lost their jobs during the preceding year (between January 1997 and 1998) three-quarters (74.1 per cent) had received no benefit at all.

Village studies reveal that informal mechanisms have cushioned the impact of the crisis. A study conducted by the International Fund for Agricultural Development (IFAD) documented support given to returning migrants by community networks, local temples and extended families. Assistance included sharing employment in non-farm enterprises and providing credit through group loans.[30] The negative effects on education and health, for example, have been lessened by family networks and community solidarity. However, as the crisis continues there is evidence that the absence of social protection systems and of adequate and comprehensive social safety nets implies high social costs, especially for women workers from the poorer parts of the population, because women are traditionally responsible for meeting their families' basic needs.

1.3 Emerging issues, lessons and recommendations

1.3.1 Ensuring employment and social justice

(a) *Macro-economic policies and employment promotion*

Rapid economic growth without appropriate employment promotion policies, human resource development (HRD) and social protection schemes leaves economies such as Thailand's vulnerable to the consequences of economic downturns. This CEPR identifies a few key areas in which employment policies can be strengthened to promote employment and social justice. While these issues are elaborated in various chapters that follow, a summary is given below.

An important part of *job creation* through enterprise promotion will be expanding micro-, small and medium-sized enterprises by providing services and infrastructure to improve productivity and profitability. Business development strategies should tap the potential of the informal sector as a provider of jobs and income. The Government has launched a job creation programme combined with community development initiatives, and as Thailand moves out of the crisis these programmes should be reassessed to gauge their contributions to sustainable employment and community development.

The *Public Employment Service* has responded remarkably well as a job placement agency. However, it will need to be strengthened to provide additional services and conduct

---

[30] D. Nathan; G. Kelkar; N. Supanchaimat. 1998. *Carrying the burden of the crisis: Women and the rural poor in Thailand*, study prepared for IFAD, cited in World Bank. 1999. *Thailand Social Monitor: Challenge for social reform* (Bangkok).

policy analysis. In particular, the internal management information system will need to be strengthened.

The social costs resulting from massive layoffs and reduced income from the economic crisis point to the need to improve *social protection and launch an unemployment insurance system*. Thailand has reached a point in its development at which such a system is affordable.

A number of questions have been raised about *minimum wages* in terms. of levels and mechanisms. Recent studies have shed light on some of the issues raised but additional information is needed to enable Thailand to select an appropriate minimum wage policy. This will require better information about decentralized wage setting and enterprise incentives.

Migration policies should be based on considerations of long-term labour market and human resource needs. These policies should also follow the principles of the Migration for Employment Convention, 1949 (No. 97), and the Migrant Workers (Supplementary Provision) Convention, 1975 (No. 143).

High priority should be given to measures aimed at eliminating *trafficking in women and children*. More generally, steps should be taken to ensure that the principles of equality and non-discriminatory treatment of women and men enshrined in law are implemented.

In order to shift the structure of output and exports to products with a higher value-added component, Thailand needs to improve *the skills of its workers* through better education and training. This requires a national strategy and coordinated policies. Developing knowledge and skills improves competitiveness and increases employability. It can also reduce poverty and promote equity.

Social dialogue leads to better employment decisions. In order to achieve this, Thailand will need to strengthen its industrial relations system through stronger tripartite machinery and bipartite relations. How well labour markets adjust to changes in supply and demand is influenced by industrial relations systems and labour market institutions.

Through its examination of these issues, the CEPR has unveiled serious weaknesses in *information and analysis* used to formulate labour market policies. The final section of this report examines suggestions for improving the labour market information system.

There is evidence that action to address the employment challenges and social impact of the economic crisis has not always reached target groups. Initiatives designed to improve targeting include revisions of the Labour Force Survey and the creation of a community unemployment register. Data from both should make it possible to direct action towards women workers and vulnerable groups. Other groups of special concern, such as disabled persons and ethnic minorities, should also be identified in data collection, as should the poor in general.

1.3.2 Building institutions toward growth, employment and social justice

(a) Democratic institutions

An ILO monograph on the financial crisis published last year stresses the importance of democratic institutions for ensuring social equity in the development process. It argues that:

The strengthening of democratic institutions is central to the post-crisis economic model that is required. Free and fair electoral processes, freedom of expression and public debate, the rule of law and accountability of elected officials are among the attributes of democracy that are essential for preventing the harmful distortion of market processes by arbitrary government intervention and corruption. The recent crisis has shown such arbitrariness to have not only economic but social costs. Thus, the intrinsic value of democracy is strongly reinforced by socio-economic conditions.[31]

These same themes are deeply embedded in the Eighth Plan and the 1997 Constitution. Implementation of reforms is under way. However, the envisioned changes may run counter to some vested interests. Thailand must move with commitment and resolve towards realizing the goals of the 1997 Constitution.

(b) Social dialogue

In terms of employment policy, social dialogue concerns the quantity and quality of jobs and efforts to strike an appropriate balance between labour market flexibility and social protection. It provides the channel through which necessary adjustments can be discussed and decided. Ideally, social dialogue increases national competitiveness by enabling employers and workers to respond quickly and effectively to shifting demand. These responses should be based on mutual benefits that can reduce bankruptcies, increase profitability, sustain employment, promote training and increase protection through providing decent work as an alternative to cheap labour, industrial conflict and work stoppages.

(c) ILO Conventions

It has been internationally accepted that freedom of association and the right to organize are basic human rights. The acceptance of these rights will lead to improvements in conditions of work. Freedom of association contributes to building democracy and fostering participation. Decisions reached by consensus between employers and workers have a greater likelihood of successful implementation. Until recently, Thailand had ratified only two of the ILO's seven core Conventions, namely the Forced Labour Convention, 1930 (No. 29), and the Abolition of Forced Labour Convention, 1957 (No. 105). However, the Government has accepted the ILO Declaration on Fundamental Principles and Rights at Work and Thailand has recently ratified the Equal Remuneration Convention, 1951 (No. 100). Thai legislation on freedom of association, though, is not in line with international standards. Efforts have been made to bring legislation closer to the internationally recognized standards on freedom of association but have failed. A number of bills have been submitted to Parliament, but due to alterations made by rapidly changing governments and slow parliamentary procedures, none has been approved. Thus, a large proportion of Thai workers remains barred from exercising their collective rights and from contributing to the country's social development.

Decent Work: The ILO seeks to promote opportunities for women and men to obtain decent and productive work in conditions of freedom, equity, security and human dignity. It is concerned with all workers, including those who are unemployed and those who are employed, those engaged in informal activities as well as those employed in the formal sector. Decent work includes possibilities for work and rights at work, quality of employment as well as quantity of jobs. It involves basic security in the midst of changing circumstances, the provision of social protection as well as the promotion of social dialogue. Based on consultations with the government, employers and workers, this CEPR aims to guide Thailand in the direction of achieving decent work for all.

---

[31] Eddy Lee. 1998. *The Asian financial crisis: The challenge for social policy* (Geneva, ILO).

Chapter 2

Enterprise policies and job creation

It was explained in Chapter 1 that rapid growth of the economy was instrumental in leading Thailand to almost full employment conditions. In the process, the economy diversified, with the small and medium-sized enterprise sector playing a major role. This chapter looks at the role that enterprise policies can play in promoting growth, employment and decent work opportunities within a context of competitiveness. It also examines the role and commitment of Government. The second part of the chapter looks at Government responses to the financial crisis and special employment-creation programmes put together in its wake. The increasingly important role played by employment services in layoff management and job placement is highlighted in the last section.

2.1 Enterprise development policies

2.1.1 Scope and role of the small enterprise sector

The predominance of small-scale enterprises in Thailand can be seen in the results of the National Statistical Office's 1996 survey.[1] Of the 157,363 enterprises included in the survey, 74.7 per cent employ one to four workers; 94.2 per cent employ one to 19 workers and 97.2 per cent employ one to 49 workers (see Table 2.1). This information provides an indication of the scale and scope of the "micro- and small enterprise sector". It is further estimated that four or five times as many unregistered enterprises have not been included in this survey,[2] leading to an estimated number of between 600,000-800,000 enterprises. The vast majority of these would, of course, be micro- and small enterprises (MSEs).

Various estimates[3] have been made of the contributions that small and medium-sized enterprises (SMEs) make to "gross output", "value-added" and "gross receipts" based on National Statistical Office data. While SME contributions to gross output and value-added in the manufacturing sector are relatively modest (respectively 6 per cent and 8.2 per cent), they are substantial in the business sector (including trade and services) at 58.9 per cent for gross receipts and 47.5 per cent for value-added. If the industrial and business sectors are assessed together, it can be shown that the SME sector's contribution to value-added is 20 per cent. These estimated contributions are probably lower than the actual values since they do not cover non-registered enterprises. Moreover, some proportion of the contribution made by small enterprises through subcontracting will have been attributed to (relatively more substantial) medium-sized and large enterprises in the statistics.

---

[1] NSO. 1998. *Report of the 1996 listing of industrial and business establishments – Whole Kingdom* (Bangkok).

[2] Allal makes this estimate based on NSO. 1996. *Formal and informal labour force market: Labour force survey, 1994* (Bangkok). See M. Allal. 1999. *Micro- and small enterprises in Thailand: Definitions and contributions*, Working Paper 6 for the ILO/UNDP Project on Micro- and Small Enterprise Development and Poverty Alleviation in Thailand: THA/99/003 (Bangkok, ILO/EASMAT).

[3] NSO. 1996. *Report of the 1995 business, trade and services survey – Whole Kingdom* (Bangkok).

Table 2.1: Number and percentage of enterprises for each enterprise size

(Number and per cent)

Manufacturing sub-sector	Total manu-facturing	Size of enterprises (number of persons engaged per establishment)								
		1-4	5-9	10-19	20-49	50-99	100-199	200-499	500-999	1,000+
Total per size of enterprise	157,363 (100)	117,588 (74.7)	21,666 (13.8)	8,897 (5.7)	4,662 (3.0)	1,896 (1.2)	1,195 (0.8)	878 (0.6)	367 (0.23)	219 (0.14)
Food, beverages and tobacco	23,827 (15.2)	18,502 (15.7)	3,091 (14.3)	1,193 (13.4)	554 (11.9)	196 (10.3)	118 (9.9)	97 (11.0)	51 (13.9)	25 (11.4)
Textile, garments leather and leather goods	64,637 (41.1)	54,609 (46.4)	5,713 (26.4)	2,141 (24.1)	1,056 (22.7)	456 (24.1)	285 (23.8)	226 (25.7)	91 (24.8)	60 (27.4)
Wood, furniture and wood products	15,002 (9.5)	12,019 (10.2)	1,571 (7.3)	726 (8.2)	385 (8.3)	127 (1.4)	89 (7.4)	55 (6.3)	21 (5.7)	9 (4.1)
Paper, printing and publishing	5,944 (3.8)	2,944 (2.5)	1,551 (7.3)	791 (8.9)	383 (8.3)	136 (1.9)	72 (6.0)	37 (4.2)	19 (5.2)	11 (5.0)
Chemicals, coal rubber and petroleum	4,733 (3.0)	1,781 (1.5)	871 (4.0)	749 (8.4)	578 (12.4)	302 (15.9)	215 (18.0)	159 (18.1)	60 (16.3)	18 (8.2)
Non-metallic mineral products	5,205 (3.3)	3,086 (2.6)	1,142 (5.3)	502 (5.6)	247 (5.3)	112 (5.9)	52 (4.4)	36 (4.2)	20 (5.4)	8 (3.7)
Basic metal industries	1,291 (0.8)	757 (0.6)	230 (1.0)	114 (1.3)	90 (2.0)	48 (2.5)	26 (2.2)	14 (1.6)	7 (1.9)	5 (2.3)
Machinery, metal products, equipment	28,406 (18.1)	17,692 (15.0)	6,300 (29.1)	2,246 (25.2)	1,135 (24.3)	421 (22.2)	262 (21.2)	196 (22.3)	86 (23.4)	68 (31.1)
Other industries	8,318 (5.3)	6,198 (5.4)	1,197 (5.5)	435 (4.9)	234 (5.1)	98 (5.0)	76 (6.4)	53 (6.0)	12 (3.3)	15 (6.8)

Source: NSO. 1998. Report of the 1996 listing of industrial and business establishments – Whole Kingdom, (Bangkok).

Note: The percentages express the number of establishments in each enterprise size category as a percentage of the total number of establishments.

In Thailand, all micro-enterprises are also generally included under the term "small enterprises" although it is useful to make a distinction between them for policy purposes. The present system of enterprise classification is also not satisfactory. Clear definitions would make it easier to identify target groups and help ensure that support services are delivered to the intended beneficiaries. A recent ILO/UNDP study on micro- and small enterprises in Thailand has proposed a methodology for improving the current classification.[4] Essentially, this would involve identifying enterprises in terms of selected criteria – the number of employees and the value of fixed assets or the turnover. On this basis, enterprises can be classified into four sizes: micro, small, medium-sized and large. As a working definition for this chapter, we use the term micro-enterprises to refer to businesses with one to four workers – although some countries include all enterprises with less than ten workers in this category. Another important but difficult to define term is the informal sector. According to the 15th International Conference of Labour Statisticians (ILO, 1993), an informal sector enterprise is "a private non-agricultural business which is household-operated and has a total of, at most, five paid employees".

This overview of the SME sector demonstrates that any form of development support to the SME sector in Thailand is justified, not only in terms of its important contribution to employment, but also its contribution to other economic objectives, such as economic growth, value-added and exports, particularly through subcontracting. In addition, measures to increase the productivity of the sector will have a significant impact on its manufacturing and trade links with larger enterprises, while also helping Thai industries face the challenge of global competition.

2.1.2 Government support for enterprise development

The Royal Thai Government has assigned considerable priority to promoting and developing small and medium-sized enterprises in the expectation that the sector can make a positive contribution to economic growth and to overcoming the adverse effects of the financial crisis.

The support programmes normally provided to promote enterprise development can be divided into two categories. The first, business development services, includes all non-financial support services such as programmes providing information, training and advice. The second, financial services, refers to direct financial support for new and growing businesses.[5]

The Government's major strategy in support of the small and medium industry sector is the Industrial Master Plan, coordinated by the Ministry of Industry. Since late 1998, the Royal Thai Government has been formulating policy measures and related support mechanisms to promote SME development in Thailand, including support for industry and trade and service sectors. However, as in the past, much of the emphasis appears to be on formal and larger enterprises, including those with a workforce of up to 200 persons and with fixed assets of up to 100 million baht. The smaller and less formal enterprises still appear to be omitted from the Government support plans – inadvert as this may be. These enterprises also suffer from the *laissez faire* approach of some policy makers, who feel that informal sector and micro-enterprises can look

---

[4] Allal. 1999. op. cit.

[5] A review was recently carried out of existing institutional provisions for small enterprise development, with particular emphasis on the provision of financial and non-financial (business development services) support, as well as the relevance of international best practices in this field to the Thai context. This review comprises five working papers produced under the ILO/UNDP project on Micro- and Small Enterprise Development and Poverty Alleviation in Thailand: THA/99/003.

after themselves. Furthermore, as mentioned above, the distinctions between "micro", "small" and "medium" enterprises are not clearly defined.

The Board of Investment within the Office of the Prime Minister is the principal government agency providing incentives to stimulate investment in Thailand. However, many of the Board's activities appear oriented towards foreign investors and the development of medium and large-scale commercial and industrial operations, and therefore have little direct impact upon micro- and small enterprises.

The main institution involved in the development of micro, small or medium-sized enterprises in Thailand is the Department of Industrial Promotion (DIP) within the Ministry of Industry. The Department's mandate includes recommending policies and measures to promote small and medium-sized industries (SMIs) – as opposed to the broader range of enterprises – in accordance with the National Economic and Social Development Plan, Government policies and changes in the global economy. The DIP has translated this mandate into a threefold mission incorporating policies to develop and improve the capabilities of SMIs and the development of skilled personnel for the industrial sector, especially in technology and management, in order to upgrade productivity to meet international standards. The Department provides financial assistance, training, information, consulting and extension services and research. It also supports rural-based cottage and handicraft industries. In April 1999, the Cabinet approved the establishment of an Institute for SME Development, which may take over some of the major functions of the DIP, particularly in the areas of training and consulting. The new emphasis on "enterprise" rather than "industry" is welcome.

The Cabinet approved in principle the draft SME Promotion Bill on 22 December 1998. Its key provisions include upgrading the capabilities and efficiency of SMEs; supporting and promoting decentralized SME development to reach rural areas and communities; and developing and strengthening the DIP to make it a more capable and efficient promoter of SMEs. The Bill provides, among other things, for the establishment of an inter-ministerial SME Development Committee, and the creation of an Office of SME Development. This office would be responsible for setting, coordinating and monitoring SME policy, and administering a 5,000 million baht SME development fund. The fund would support the work of the Office of SME Development, and provide direct support to SMEs to help them to improve their productivity.[6]

Traditionally, the DIP's policies and support programmes have focused on small and medium-sized enterprises in the manufacturing sector, many of which could be classified as modern, export-oriented formal enterprises. In most cases these are also members of various employers' organizations, such as trade or sectoral associations or chambers of commerce. In contrast, insufficient institutional support has been provided for those enterprises at the smaller

---

[6] The SME Promotion Bill also calls for an SME Development Plan covering financial assistance programmes; SMEs' financial and capital markets; HRD; research; development and technology transfer within the sector; product development and the promotion of product standards; marketing assistance; managerial systems development; information assistance, including information technology; links with large-scale enterprises; promotion of SME associations, provincial and regional SME development, promotion of NGOs that support SME development; infrastructure for SME investments; incentives to compensate for the disadvantages and limitations of SMEs; environmental and occupational hazards; and other issues related to strengthening SMEs and improving their competitiveness.

end of the spectrum, many of which employ less than ten persons. These enterprises can be classified as informal or micro-enterprises, and are often engaged in trading and services.

In all, 18 organizations are involved in the development of micro-, small and medium-sized enterprises in Thailand, including four government ministries. The existing network of government departments and parastatal organisations is sufficient to regulate and monitor development of the SME sector. However, their centralized structure and their location in large bureaucracies makes it difficult for them to reach entrepreneurs, particularly micro-enterprises.[7] Since the onset of the financial crisis, more Government ministries, including the Ministry of the Interior and Ministry of Labour and Social Welfare, have also become significant players in supporting micro-enterprises and community development. Even so, they are not involved in the new SME Development Committee. Limited participation by the private sector and member-based associations in development programmes also needs to be improved.

The crisis and its legacy of financial institution closures and non-performing loans have placed pressure on remaining institutions and left them wary of lending risks. A review of financial support found that there is a sufficient number and range of financial institutions in Thailand to provide support services to small and medium-sized enterprises. However, these institutions have proved less capable and willing micro-enterprises. Conventional lending practices and the role played by personal connections and influence account for much of this, as well as the institutions' collateral requirements. Together with the poor networks and inadequate capital of many micro-enterprise operators, this has severely limited their access to financial resources. The Royal Thai Government plans to address this by means of two new finance windows for the micro-enterprise sector. While details are yet to be released, it is understood that they will be oriented towards profitable and sustainable enterprises, with Government Savings Banks serving clients in the urban areas, and the Bank of Agriculture and Agricultural Cooperatives covering the rural areas. Linking supportive financial services with business development services is also important. So, too, is developing the capacities of the funding institutions to serve these micro-enterprises effectively.

2.1.3 The urban informal sector

A National Statistical Office survey of the informal sector (NSO, 1996) indicates that this sector plays a major role as a source of employment for millions of people and contributes to the achievement of a number of socio-economic objectives.[8] More than three-quarters of the employed labour force is in the informal sector. The informal sector, moreover, accounts for 52 per cent of enterprises in the manufacturing, trade and service sectors. Using the Office's 1997 statistics on industrial and business establishments, employment generated by the informal sector in the manufacturing, trade and service sectors[9] is approximately 3.5 times greater than

---

[7] ILO/UNDP project documentation shows that at best 2 per cent of the DIP's target group are being served [Allal. op. cit.].

[8] The findings from this survey are corroborated by various studies, most notably two studies carried out by the ILO. 1995a. *An enabling policy framework for the urban informal sector, Thailand* (Bangkok, ILO) and 1993b. *Dynamism in the informal sector in a fast growing economy: The case of Bangkok* (New Delhi, ILO-ARTEP).

[9] It should be noted that the informal sector is not clearly defined in Thailand. The definitions used by the NSO and others are based on qualitative characteristics of the sector and on the number of employees (one to nine workers according to the NSO definition). These definitions could equally apply to formally registered micro-enterprises.

that generated by the formal sector.[10] In terms of job creation, the contribution made by informal sector enterprises involved in trading is much more important than that of the manufacturing and service sectors. Women are also more represented in the informal than the formal sector; 1994 NSO data indicate that 47 per cent of all workers in the informal sector are women, while they account for 43 per cent of the formal sector workers.

2.1.4 Recommendations

(a) *The need for overall policy coordination and support of SMEs*

The Royal Thai Government should strive to improve cooperation and coordination between all of the key players engaged in promoting and supporting enterprise development, including economic and non-economic ministries, the private sector and the NGO community. Involving the Ministry of Labour and Social Welfare and the Ministry of the Interior in new institutions such as the Institute for Small and Medium Enterprise Development would help to achieve this. In addition, there is scope for improving collaboration within ministries such as the Ministry of Labour and Social Welfare. This Ministry in particular should establish a coordinating team of enterprise focal persons comprised of representatives of units (from various departments) actively involved in promoting, developing and supporting enterprise creation and development. This team could also advocate Ministry policies and approaches in support of enterprises to other line ministries.

The forthcoming SME Promotion Act appears to continue the trend of promoting businesses at the larger end of the scale. It overlooks many of the needs, potential and scope for development of self-employment and micro-enterprises. Better recognition of the micro-, small and medium-sized sector is needed, and of its potential for contributing to national development goals, together with a broader policy framework with a new, more inclusive orientation. Comprehensive support and business development services should be provided, as well as initiatives targeting SMEs operating within specific sectors (e.g. tourism and export-oriented enterprises). Measures are also needed to review, assess and improve the operational environment of the sector and market linkages between micro- and small enterprises and larger ones. In addition, mechanisms should be created to monitor and measure the outreach and impact of all support programmes.

A policy framework is needed that provides motivation and direction for strengthening and expanding the SME sector. The ILO's Recommendation concerning General Conditions to Stimulate Job Creation in Small and Medium-sized Enterprises, 1998 (No. 189) – which has recently been translated into Thai – as well as its International Small Enterprise Programme have much to contribute to key implementing partners in Thailand.

(b) *Greater support for micro-enterprises*

While the need to develop the overall SME sector is not disputed, there appears to be a gap in the provision of services by Government which has left the micro-enterprises isolated from support and recognition by the economic line ministries. Thus, they must rely on the welfare-oriented support services of the social ministries. The latter form of support has been provided on the basis of welfare criteria and measures of disadvantage, rather than economic potential. Much of the earlier enterprise development and support effort has focused on the larger SMEs,

---

[10] Allal. 1999. op. cit.

frequently leaving the micro-enterprises to fend for themselves. Many efforts to develop micro-enterprises in Thailand have been based on welfare models of support, rather than models that promote and enhance the entrepreneurial capacity of the sector. The various government ministries and departments responsible for working with poverty affected groups (e.g. the Departments of Skills Development, Employment and Public Welfare in the Ministry of Labour and Social Welfare, and the Community Development Department in the Ministry of the Interior) should be provided with skills and methodologies for promoting and supporting enterprises, to ensure that they do not rely on welfare or dependency-based models.

As in many developing countries, as few as 10 per cent of Thailand's informal or micro-enterprises are likely to graduate into small formal enterprises. However, support policies that could increase the graduation rate (even by 1 or 2 per cent) will have a significant impact given the large numbers of micro-enterprises. In addition, it is likely that informal sector enterprises will remain informal for as long as the benefits (both tangible and perceived) of formal status do not outweigh the costs measured in financial, administrative and other significant terms. Programmes to support informal sector enterprises should enable them to graduate, so that they ultimately become formal tax-paying units that comply with various legal requirements.

The mechanisms for effecting policy changes, implementing new programmes and creating new institutions in relation to small enterprise development should take account of international best practices, with particular emphasis on experiences from the regional groupings with which Thailand is affiliated. This could include promoting member-based associations of micro- and small entrepreneurs, as well as institution-building programmes to develop their capacity as service providers to their membership.

There should be a shift in overall emphasis away from relying solely on financial support mechanisms to supporting business development services, particularly through private sector service providers. Furthermore, more attention should be devoted to improving the productivity, profitability, employment potential and income-generating potential of the service and trade sectors. This could be achieved by promoting specific trade and service sectors, such as information and communications technologies, personal health-care services and eco-tourism, as well as by encouraging the formation of sector-based associations in new and emerging sectors. The employers' organizations have reinforced the importance of basic business management skills for small enterprises and endorsed the value and relevance of the ILO's Start and Improve Your Business materials, which are currently being adapted for use in Thailand.

(c)   Carry out a study of the informal sector based on a survey

Given the importance of the informal sector in the Thai economy, it is recommended that the National Statistical Office conduct a special informal sector survey based on a "mixed" sample of households and establishments, in accordance with international standards.[11] Almost all the constituents consulted in the process of conducting this review identified the informal sector as a major information gap. Improvements have been introduced to the Labour Force Survey to provide information on informal sector employment. It is, however, recommended that a separate informal sector survey disaggregated by sex be conducted to provide more detailed data. This survey could draw on the guidelines established for informal sector statistics

---

[11] A sample of households is used to identify persons who work in the informal sector. Information on the informal sector enterprise is then used as a second sampling frame. From this a sample of workplaces is obtained.

by the 15th International Conference of Labour Statisticians (ILO, 1993a), and the ILO Labour Statistics Convention, 1985 (No. 160). A survey would enable policymakers to identify ways to design effective policies and support programmes for male and female workers in the informal sector as well as to encourage decent work through better working conditions.

It is also apparent that a large number of women are engaged in the informal sector – many as home-workers – as well as in micro-enterprise trading and service activities. However, little is known about their economic, working and social conditions or their access to productive and financial resources. An in-depth study is recommended to identify the barriers and constraints facing women in the informal sector and micro-enterprises.

These surveys should be designed in consultation with various users of the statistics including the National Statistical Office, the Ministry of Labour and Social Welfare, the Ministry of Industry, the Ministry of Commerce, the National Economic and Social Development Board and the Thailand Development Research Institute, together with academic institutions, employers' and workers' organizations and concerned NGOs.

2.2 Social investment and job creation programmes

The Eighth National Economic and Social Development Plan (1996-2000) was drawn up at a time of high economic growth and labour shortages. The Plan focused on reducing regional disparities and promoting equity. It assumed that high growth would continue at 8 per cent per annum, and emphasized the need to correct the unsustainable trend towards rural poverty and growing income disparities. Hence, it advocated administrative decentralization, strengthening of communities and people-centred development. The economic crisis, however, led to negative growth and substantial job losses in all sectors, and posed a new challenge for the rural sector to absorb the many laid-off workers who returned from the cities.

Major international donors and the development banks have provided loan assistance for social investment programmes to cushion the impact of the crisis. First, these have provided additional resources for increasing productive capacity, largely through infrastructure investments. Second, they are meant to address growing unemployment problems with job-creation initiatives. Third, these programmes aim to support the Government's reform agenda, contributing to decentralization, capacity building, and community development. The key issue is whether the three objectives can effectively be combined.

Thailand has its own history of job creation programmes. A variety of initiatives have been launched over the three decades or so from the 1960s till the early 1990s. Most of these programmes were initiated and supported by central government, and implemented through technical line departments. Project preparation and implementation was decentralized to local levels in some cases. The Rural Job Creation Programme and the Tambon Development Programme are examples. Assessments of these programmes have given them a weak to moderate rating in terms of targeting the poor but acknowledged that they had better success in improving distribution of incomes in target areas.[12] On balance, direct job-creation objectives seem to have predominated at the expense of enhancing productive capacity. In the final phases of the programmes, which coincided with the economic boom of the early 1990s, an expanding

---

[12] Medhi Krongkaew. 1997. *Poverty Alleviation through public works: Cases of the Rural Job Creation Program, the Green Isarn Program, and the Tambon Development Program*, Paper prepared for the World Bank, (Bangkok, World Bank Office Thailand, unpublished).

private contracting sector had gradually substituted heavy equipment for local unskilled labour. Under central and provincial Government direction, the emphasis on labour-intensive strategies was reduced. Employment generated by these schemes dropped sharply. For example, in 1980 more than 3.7 million rural workers were engaged in the Rural Job Creation Programme whereas only 142,302 workers were employed throughout the country in 1991. In 1990 the requirement that a minimum 70 per cent of the project budget should be used for labour and local resources was dropped.

Following the crisis, there have been a number of ongoing efforts to promote job creation among specific groups and within local communities. The major target groups for the social investment programmes are retrenched workers, the poor, home workers and unemployed youth. This section does not cover the activities of numerous NGOs, which may have a bearing on job creation. Many NGOs and community-based organizations are at present involved in either government-initiated or donor-initiated programmes. The information base on existing programmes for employment generation is inadequate, due, in part, to the fact that the programmes have been launched only recently. It also reflects the lack of coordination among the many actors involved and the absence of mechanisms for monitoring the employment impact. Better information is available on financial allocations rather than on the number of jobs to be created and the actual employment impact.

2.2.1 Review of policies and programmes

Wide publicity has been given to the seven-point Action Plan for Unemployment Relief announced by the Government in November 1997. The following seven measures aim to generate 1.48 million jobs using a budget of 61.4 billion baht:[13]

(i)   the "Thai Help Thai" promotion of social assistance, designed to provide cheap consumer products and loans for self-employment through the efforts of communities supported by line agencies;

(ii)   rural employment promotion, for which the Government set a target of 350,000 temporary positions for unemployed persons in 1998. All ministries and line agencies were advised to use their annual budget for labour-intensive projects;

(iii)   industrial employment promotion, sustaining employment in the industrial sector by providing micro-credit for the self-employed and organizing training programmes;

(iv)   immigrant workers' replacement, involving strict control and repatriation of migrant workers in Thailand, especially undocumented workers so as to save around 300,000 jobs for local workers;

(v)   promotion of labour exports, with mention of a target of 210,000-250,000 workers and a range of government incentives and services including loans for prospective migrants;

(vi)   promotion of the New Agricultural Model proposed by His Majesty the King based on self-sufficiency and environment preservation concepts which aim to return workers to the rural areas;

(vii)   employment access promotion, advocating an information centre concerned with job opportunities and career and occupational guidance for new graduates and laid-off workers.

---

[13] C. Boonpratuang. 1999. *A review of action on employment relief*, NESDB paper for the ILO Asian Regional Consultation on Follow-Up to the World Summit for Social Development (Bangkok, ILO/ROAP).

The Government has underlined its commitment by setting up a high-level National Unemployment Alleviation Policy Committee chaired by the Prime Minister, with representatives of concerned ministries and the Ministry of Labour and Social Welfare as the secretariat. There is however, limited information on the impact of these measures.

Moreover, there are special programmes operated by various ministries. For instance, the Ministry of Labour and Social Welfare and its departments, and the Ministry of the Interior and its various arms including the Department of Local Administration, the Public Works Department and the Department of Community Development, carry out a number of job-creation programmes.

The ILO has been involved in assessing the feasibility of introducing an unemployment insurance scheme.[14]

2.2.2 Initiatives by donors and development banks

There are three major donor and development bank funded initiatives: the Social Investment Programme, with major funding from the World Bank; the Miyazawa Plan (funded by the Government of Japan and the World Bank); and the Asian Development Bank's Social Sector Programme Loan. While the emphasis of the programmes is on public investments in the broader sense and on the social sectors of education, health and labour/employment, the programmes attempt to combine long-term considerations of capacity building and competitiveness with short-term assistance for job creation.

(a) Social Investment Programme

The Social Investment Programme brings together funding of US$462 million, with contributions from the World Bank ($300 million), the Overseas Economic Co-operation Fund of Japan ($123 million) and the Government of Thailand ($49 million). The programme's first objective is to remedy immediate problems including unemployment and the fall in the standard of living among laid-off workers and the unemployed. It provides support to the unemployed and vulnerable groups affected by the crisis through access to employment opportunities, skill development and basic social services. The second objective is longer term. The programme supports the Government's agenda for public and administrative reform, contributing to sustainable development through capacity building and strengthening planning, service delivery, and people's participation at the local levels.

Social Investment Programme projects are split into two channels matching the above objectives. The first channel covers government and public sector enterprise projects which had been postponed due to budget constraints. The projects span a wide variety of line ministry projects, with emphasis on public infrastructure under the Ministry of the Interior and the Bangkok Metropolitan Administration, and special projects under the Ministry of Health and the Ministry of Labour and Social Welfare. This last is primarily responsible for providing training to three target groups: unemployed persons; disadvantaged women and disabled persons; and women and youth. The Ministry of the Interior programme's objectives include creating employment opportunities and improving basic infrastructure and services in rural areas. According to the World Bank, these projects should rapidly create employment opportunities in rural areas, which faced inflows of returning migrants who had lost jobs in urban areas. In

---

[14] See ILO. 1998c. *Thailand: Assessment of the feasibility of introducing an unemployment insurance scheme in Thailand: Report to the Government* (Geneva, Social Security Department).

addition, they should help improve rural infrastructure. These projects must be completed within 28 months of their late-1998 starting date.

To ensure sustainable development through community building and to strengthen local-level participation, the Social Investment Programme has set up two funds running projects over a period of 40 months. The first is the US$120 million Social Investment Fund, designed (i) to improve access for poor people to basic social and economic infrastructure, services and employment opportunities; and (ii) to support bottom-up service delivery through promoting decentralization, local capacity building, and community development.[15] It provides support to communities to carry out projects in community welfare, community infrastructure, environmental protection, etc. The Government Savings Bank is responsible for disbursement, with the Social Fund Office as the fund managing arm. An update in July 1999 reported that 350 projects had been approved, with the fund disbursement reasonably on target according to the local World Bank Office. The second is the Regional Urban Development Fund, with US$30 million. The emphasis is on the improvement of basic infrastructure, facilities and services, and creating employment in strategically important urban centres outside Bangkok. Only two projects worth 47.5 million baht had been approved by May 1999.

(b) Miyazawa Loan Fund

The Miyazawa initiative was launched by the Government of Japan to help crisis-affected countries in Asia move towards economic recovery. In Thailand, The Miyazawa Loan Fund aims to stimulate economic recovery through investments, alleviate the adverse social impact of the economic crisis and create a framework for sustainable development (see Table 2.2). Public infrastructure is presented as an important instrument for job creation and accounts for a major share of the budget. The Fund specifies that at least 20 billion baht (some 38 per cent of the total) should be set aside for job creation and assistance for the disadvantaged. A target of 486,000 new jobs, primarily in rural communities, has been set. Fund conditions stipulate that wage rates for workers should be in line with existing rates in rural areas. This is important to ensure decent wages. Building administrative efficiency represents a special project category with funding of 8 billion baht. This category includes an operation designed to decentralize responsibilities to the locally-administered Tambon level.

(c) The Asian Development Bank's Social Sector Programme Loan

This loan has both long-term and short-term components covering the labour, education and health sectors. Of relevance to job creation are components dealing with computer training for 10,000 retrenched/unemployed workers with upper secondary level education, improving labour force information and community strengthening through employment-creation projects. Most programmes had been launched in early 1999.

2.2.3 An assessment of job creation programmes

A systematic assessment of the impact of projects carried out under these loan programmes is not available, in part because planning has only recently been completed. However, some difficulties in project implementation have surfaced, among them long delays in disbursing funds. These delays are largely due to problems with coordination between different ministries.

---

[15] IBRD. 1998. Report No. 17785TH, Project appraisal document on a proposed loan in the amount of US$300 million to the Kingdom of Thailand for a Social Investment Project, 15 June 1998 (Health, Nutrition and Population Sector Unit, East Asia and Pacific Region).

Table 2.2: Projects under the Miyazawa Initiative

Item of expenditure	Million baht	Per cent of total
1. Investment and job creation aimed at alleviating the social impact of the economic crisis	24,827	46.4
1.1 Job creation	22,706	42.5
Employment creation (educated workers)	4,323	8.1
Employment creation (unskilled workers)	18,383	34.4
1.2 Expansion of investment	771	1.4
1.3 Alleviation of the economic hardship of the poor	1,350	2.5
2. Improvement in quality of life	9,565	17.9
2.1 Public health	5,012	9.4
2.2 Pollution and environment management	2,235	4.2
2.3 Water resource management	2,318	4.3
3. Improvements in the economic foundation		
3.1 Minimization of the impact of the economic crisis on education	7,009	13.1
3.2 Improving agriculture and manufacturing production	2,665	5.0
3.3 Stabilization of commodity prices	344	0.6
4. Improvement in the competitiveness of manufacturing and export industries	2,330	4.4
5. Improvement in basic infrastructure and the development of specific areas	867	1.6
6. Enhancing the effectiveness of public administration	8,800	16.5
Total	53,398	100.0

Source: Department of Fiscal Economics, Ministry of Finance.

The sudden and simultaneous increase in the scale of activities carried out by many line agencies and the short project timeframes led to shortages of qualified personnel to handle the projects. The conditions set by the Social Investment Fund were initially found to be too strict for local communities, demonstrated by the fact that of 5,000 submissions, only 235 projects had been approved by May 1999.[16] The situation is improving and approvals of Social Investment Programme projects were reported to be on target in mid-August 1999.[17] Further project implementation difficulties include the danger of duplication, overlapping mandates and mistargeting arising from simultaneous launches of projects by different agencies. There are reports that quick disbursement of funds has resulted in leakage and corruption.[18] For the projects under line ministries, it seems that job-creation potential has not been adequately explored in the rush to disburse funds. This is the case with infrastructure projects where the most appropriate labour-based methods have not been considered, mainly due to the lack of guidelines for the involvement of local labour. World Bank and ILO missions in August 1999 reported that Social Investment Fund construction projects were involving, on average, more than 50 per cent of the

---

[16] Arya Gosah. 1999. *Economic crisis employment and labour market in Thailand*, Report prepared for the ILO/EASMAT (Bangkok, unpublished).

[17] Communication by ILO ASIST-AP on the basis of local World Bank Office information.

[18] EIU. 1999. *Country report, Thailand, 3rd Quarter*, cited in Bangkok Post, 7 June 1999.

labour available in the community in which they operated. However, the fact that the project appraisal forms do not require information on targeted workdays of employment or duration of jobs created may act as a constraint on greater use of labour by implementing agencies. There are mixed reports on the performance of the Miyazawa Plan projects.

These include accounts of contractors relying on capital-intensive approaches and communities therefore missing out on expected benefits in the form of wage labour. Finally, while the emphasis on local capacity building and community development is to be welcomed, to be effective, these efforts must continue well beyond the project's completion date. A proper balance must be struck between quick disbursement of funds (such as through traditional capital-intensive contracting) and a slower, more targeted disbursement (through smaller implementation units, such as communities or small contractors) if long-term goals of capacity building and local development are to be achieved.

2.2.4 Policy recommendations

The key policy recommendation is building the capacity of communities and implementing agencies to identify, design, implement, monitor and evaluate income-and employment-generation projects.

(a) *Community-driven, sustainable, and income- and employment-generation projects to help the poor and vulnerable groups*

In line with the Eighth Plan objectives of people's empowerment and decentralization, current policy has focused on community participation and initiatives. The National Social Policy Committee has established a Community Empowerment for Response to Crisis Action Plan to empower communities to respond to the effects of the crisis. The Ministry of Labour and Social Welfare and the Ministry of the Interior also have programmes which reach down to the community levels. Promoting community participation requires:

(i)   community needs assessments to establish priorities;

(ii)   improving information collection at the local level by coordinating efforts such as the Community Unemployment Register, the Unemployed Graduates Programme and village welfare centres;

(iii) linking local employment- and income-generation programmes to avoid overlapping and duplication;

(iv)   providing skills and management training for community leaders and target groups;

(v)   promoting participatory approaches;

(vi)   promoting self-employment through community-based micro-credit schemes, aimed particularly at women workers affected by the crisis;

(vii) establishing revolving funds to sustain employment-creation and income-generation schemes.

(b) *Capacity building of government agencies involved in local level planning*

Government agencies need to improve their capacity in several areas: identification and design, targeting, implementation, monitoring and evaluation of sustainable income-generation and employment programmes. Given the vital role played by the rural sector in absorbing labour, including laid-off urban workers, both public sector and private agencies handling infrastructure investment programmes need to be made more aware of labour-based approaches. Unless these approaches are used, the programmes' employment potential will not be realized. As the Social Investment Fund experience showed, implementing agencies need training in project appraisal and management. There is a considerable body of knowledge and international experience in these areas which Thailand can draw upon. The detailed results of the Labour Force Survey and the Community Unemployment Register initiative of the Asian Development Bank's Social Sector Programme Loan should help identify priority areas and groups. Monitoring and evaluation is another weak area in which international agencies might usefully assist. The UNDP and Australian Agency for International Development are already providing support for monitoring and evaluation of the Miyazawa Plan.

(c) Involve employers' and workers' organizations in social investment programmes

Employers' and workers' organizations need to be involved in social investment and job-creation programmes. At present, these programmes are mainly implemented by government line agencies, NGO networks and community-based organizations. Workers' and employers' representatives could help identify target groups and assist with project development, monitoring and evaluation.

2.3 Employment services

2.3.1 The Public Employment Service

Thailand has ratified the ILO Employment Service Convention, 1949 (No. 88). The Department of Employment within the Ministry of Labour and Social Welfare is responsible for all employment services provided by public and private organizations, whether for domestic or overseas placements. The Public Employment Service (PES) is responsible for:

(i)   providing free public labour exchange, employment counselling and guidance services in 75 provinces and the Bangkok area;

(ii)   undertaking labour market research and analysis designed to facilitate the provision of employment services and the formulation of employment policy;

(iii) maintaining national standard occupational and industrial classifications;

(iv)   developing systems, formats, measures and methods for providing employment services, including formulating and coordinating operational plans to be carried out by the employment services offices network.

Further regulatory services include:

(i)   registration, licensing and supervision of private employment agencies in both domestic and overseas placement of Thai nationals;

(ii)   determination of applications from foreigners for the issue or renewal of permits to engage in paid employment in Thailand;

(iii) action to ensure that foreign workers do not work illegally in Thailand.

At the central level, the Department of Employment has seven operational or functional divisions (employment services, employment promotion, labour market administration, foreign workers control, overseas employment administration, overseas placement and inspection and job seekers protection); a legal affairs division; and four administrative divisions (office of the secretary, technical and planning division; personnel division and computer administration centre). At the regional level, six labour market information centres coordinate, collect and analyse statistical reports from the employment services offices within their region.

At the district level, the Department has a network of 84 local employment services offices (one in each of the 75 provinces and nine in the Bangkok area). In addition, there are 11 overseas employment check points which review the bona fides of migrant workers' contracts and advise workers on assistance avenues overseas. Each local office has two main operational sections. The employment promotion section deals with labour exchange, job search assistance and other labour market adjustment programmes. The employment protection section issues and supervises work permits for foreigners; supervises private employment agencies (domestic and overseas); and in some cases the placement of workers in overseas jobs. This twin structure reflects the Department's dual role.

The number of job seekers and vacancies registered (using both flow and stock data) as well as the labour market share of the PES are often used as the indicators of PES performance. The service's labour market share is measured by comparing the percentage of PES registered job seekers to the total number of labour market job seekers, or the percentage of PES vacancies to total labour market vacancies, or the percentage of PES placements to total labour market hiring. However, in practice, all of these measures are affected by problems of definition and calculation. A recent ILO study focusing on employment services in Thailand has identified several deficiencies in the registration, calculation and publication of details relating to job seekers, job vacancies and placement statistics.[19] Data on new applicants are incomplete because they do not include job seekers who register at job bazaars or with mobile services in remote areas. These data also exclude people who use self-service job brokering (without contacting a registering officer). Double counting can also occur if the job seekers are first registered in one province and later placed in a different province under mobility programmes. Job vacancy statistics, moreover, are heavily overstated as employers commonly lodge vacancies with more than one office.

Nevertheless the study found that the PES in Thailand has fairly good labour market penetration: the placement to job seekers ratio fell from 67 per cent in 1997 to 53 per cent in 1998 while the placement to vacancies ratio increased from 60 per cent to 80 per cent. In addition, in terms of cost per placement the PES seems to stand up quite well against private employment agencies. The cost of the PES is between 1,300 and 2,000 baht per placement, while private agencies are estimated to cost 25 per cent of one month's average salary, i.e. 1,750 baht per placement).

2.3.2 Role and performance of private employment agencies

As far as private employment services are concerned, very limited information is available.[20] At present, there are 144 private domestic agencies licensed under the Recruitment and Job Seekers Protection Act. Of these 144 agencies, only 11 are licensed to operate from

---

[19] There are other deficiencies too. For details, refer to D. Fraser. 1999. *The role of employment services in the management of the Thai labour market: A study of the recent past and possibilities for commencing the twenty-first century*, Report prepared for the MOLSW (Bangkok, ILO/EASMAT, unpublished).

[20] This excludes any consideration of the private overseas employment agencies.

bases outside Bangkok. Most of the agencies are very small and cover only one occupational group, such as housemaids or sales representatives, and make their income from charging the job seeker a fee. This fee is set by law at a maximum of 25 per cent of the first month's salary, payable after receipt the first salary payment. Based on an average wage of 7,000 baht per month, the average cost to the job seeker can be put at about 1,750 baht in 1998. The real cost of private sector placements is in fact much higher than the above figure, as it should include the costs incurred by the Department of Employment in licensing and supervising private agencies; and providing information and advisory services to potential users of private (legal and illegal) employment services. Statistically, private agencies appear to play a considerably smaller role in the overall job placement market than has generally been assumed by casual observers. Available evidence suggests that, prior to the crisis, the private sector share was about 25 per cent of that of the public sector's. In 1998 the private share appears to have totalled less than 10 per cent of the public. If these figures are even close to correct, this would mean that the share of the private domestic employment service agencies totalled less than 1 per cent of the job search market in 1998.

2.3.3 Future challenges and recommendations

During the boom period that preceded the economic crisis, the Public Employment Service's main functions were labour exchange services and producing and disseminating labour market statistics derived from its administrative records. However, the PES will need new services and tools to cope with the significant increase in employment since the crisis. The following measures are recommended:

(i)   developing the PES's capacity to monitor and evaluate the labour market adjustment programmes (e.g. training, retraining and job creation programmes) it administers. This involves improving the quality of labour market statistics derived from the PES's administrative records; training employment service staff to use other sources of labour market information and data, and to analyse and interpret these in order to trace trends in local and regional labour markets and supplement administrative data; and working towards management by objectives (setting targets, allocating resources on the basis of performance contracts, identifying and assessing performance indicators, using performance indicators to monitor the effectiveness of various PES offices);

(ii)   creating job search assistance information centres within the local employment service offices and continuing development and provision of labour exchange and other information on activities and services via the internet in order to improve labour market services;

(iii)   finding a balance between self-service labour exchange to suit general job seekers (through its recent development of job seekers and vacancies banks on computer terminals and the Internet) and more focused and intensive job search assistance for disadvantaged groups (e.g. women workers with little education or skills, the long-term unemployed, the young unemployed and disabled persons).

As the Government of Thailand is studying the possible introduction of an unemployment insurance scheme, decisions must be made concerning the involvement and integration of employment services and the social security office in administering and operating unemployment insurance, especially for the purposes of reporting and skills training This CEPR report has recommended that a thorough review of the policy and organization of unemployment insurance be undertaken (see Section 3.2.5 of Chapter 3).

Chapter 3

Social protection and unemployment benefits

Despite the rapid economic growth achieved prior to 1997, the scope of Thailand's social protection system has remained relatively limited in comparison to that of other countries with similar levels of economic development. Efforts have been made over the past decade to gradually expand social security on the basis of a comprehensive plan adopted in 1990, which essentially targets workers in formal contractual employment. However, the needs of the large number of workers outside of formal employment are still to be addressed. During the Asian financial crisis, the lack of comprehensive social protection programmes combined with inadequate administrative infrastructures made it difficult for the Government to reach out to persons in need of assistance.

Social protection systems perform two basic functions. The first is a preventive function whereby all presently and previously economically active persons build up entitlements in the event of contingencies such as unemployment, sickness, maternity, old age, invalidity and death. The second is a curative function whereby poverty is alleviated through short-term transfers, notably when there is loss of earnings. The ILO Social Security (Minimum Standards) Convention, 1951 (No. 102), provides viable proposals for a system of minimum social security protection that come within the financial capacity of countries such as Thailand.

In times of economic difficulty, there is pressure to allocate maximum resources to poverty alleviation at the expense of long-term prevention. Thailand recently experienced such pressures for implementing poverty alleviation measures, mostly through decentralized and temporary programmes of action which would mainly serve the curative function of social security.

In the course of the ILO Governing Body Symposium on The ILO's Response to the Financial Crisis in East and South-East Asia: The Social Impact of the Asian Financial Crisis, held in March 1999, a new vision for reform emerged in recognition that the deficiencies of the pre-crisis economic and social systems need to be remedied. It included the following key element: "The highest priority should be given to the strengthening of systems of social protection. Possible measures include the introduction of unemployment insurance and the expansion of social assistance schemes to relieve extreme poverty".[1] However, there are still difficulties in establishing the appropriate social dimensions of development in Thailand. When the crisis struck, the already low social security contribution rates were reduced for the period from 1998 to 2000 despite the fact that there was a need to provide benefits to unemployed workers. Nevertheless, the economic crisis has drawn attention to gaps and weaknesses in various schemes and pointed to possible strategies for strengthening the system. In the

---

[1] ILO. *Response to the financial crisis in East and South-East Asia: The social impact of the Asian financial crisis*, prepared for the ILO Governing Body Symposium, Governing Body, GB.274/4/4, 274th Session, Geneva, March 1999, p. 2.

meantime, the need for comprehensive and coordinated policies for broadening the scope and effectiveness of social protection has become increasingly recognized.[2]

3.1 The existing social protection system

3.1.1 Social Security Act, 1990

The Social Security Act, 1990 provides for the phased introduction of a comprehensive social security programme for private sector employees in respect of all seven social security contingencies, and the gradual extension of the scope of coverage of the labour force. Initially, the main benefit was comprehensive medical care which was a priority for all age groups, and was considered particularly important for the health and productivity of the workforce.

The following major steps toward establishment of the Social Security Scheme in its current form took place in line with the development of the administrative capacity of the Social Security Office (SSO).

(i)   In March 1991, the new scheme was applied to workers in establishments with 20 or more workers who were insured for sickness (medical care and cash benefits), maternity, invalidity and death.

(ii) In September 1993, employees of establishments with ten or more workers were insured.[3]

(iii) In September 1994, self-employed persons were permitted to join the SSO scheme on a voluntary basis.

(iv) In 1995, the maternity allowance was extended from 60 to 90 days, invalidity pensions became payable for life and survivors' grants were introduced.

(v)   In December 1998, old-age pensions and child allowances were introduced.

SSO benefits are financed from contributions by employees, employers and the Government. At the first stage, long-term benefits are partially funded, as contributions in a given year are collected in excess of the annual benefit expenditure. The excess amount of contributions is invested to earn interest such that a reserve fund is built up and can be used at a later stage when the scheme becomes mature and increasing numbers of insured workers become entitled to a lifetime old-age pension. The SSO provides income protection on monthly earnings of up to 15,000 baht. Contributions are earmarked for the different branches of benefits (see Table 3.1). Special measures were temporarily put into place to alleviate the burden of contributions for the years 1998 to 2000 as a result of the recent financial crisis.

Table 3.2 shows the scheduled overall rise in social security contribution rates to be collected by the SSO. But the charges for 2001 are still relatively low in comparison with

---

[2] The ILO had highlighted this in the report by Eddy Lee. 1998. *The Asian financial crisis: the challenge for social policy* (Geneva, ILO). See also, P.S. Heller. 1999. "The IMF sought to ensure that the economic policy framework could accommodate social protection measures and emphasized to the authorities that such measures should be part and parcel of IMF-supported programs," in: *Human dimensions of the Asian economic crisis*, Paper prepared for the World Bank Regional Meeting on Social Issues Arising from the East Asia Crisis and Policy Implications for the Future (Washington D.C., Fiscal Affairs Department, IMF).

[3] The extension of coverage to establishments with less than ten workers is planned at a future stage (cf. Section 3.2.1).

Table 3.1: Schedule of contribution rates to the SSO by benefit branches, (actual and planned as a percentage of insurable earnings up to 15,000 baht per month)

	1998	1999	2000	2001
Workmen's compensation benefits[a]				
– Employers[b]	0.2-1.0	0.2-1.0	0.2-1.0	0.2-1.0
– Total	0.2-1.0	0.2-1.0	0.2-1.0	0.2-1.0
Sickness, maternity, invalidity and death[c]				
– Employees	1.0	1.0	1.0	1.5
– Employers	1.0	1.0	1.0	1.5
– Government	1.0	1.0	1.0	1.5
– Total	3.0	3.0	3.0	4.5
Old age pensions and child allowance				
– Employees	...	1.0	2.0	3.0
– Employers	...	1.0	2.0	3.0
– Government	...	1.0	1.0	1.0
– Total	...	3.0	5.0	7.0

[a] When the SSO was established, it took over the administration of the Workmen's Compensation Fund.

[b] Employers' contributions to the Workmen's Compensation Fund vary according to 131 industrial classifications set on the basis of the nature of employment conditions.

[c] Between 1998 and 2000, contributions to the Social Security Fund (sickness, maternity, invalidity and death) were temporarily reduced in response to the financial crisis.

Table 3.2: Schedule of total contribution rates to the Social Security Office, 1999-2001

(As a percentage of insurable earnings up to 15,000 baht monthly)

Year	Employees	Employers[a]	Government	Total[a]
1999	2.0	2.0	2.0	6.0
2000	3.0	3.0	2.0	8.0
2001	4.5	4.5	2.5	11.5

Source: Social Security Law. 1999. (Bangkok, Social Security Office).

[a] Employers are also liable for paying additional contributions to the Workmen's Compensation Fund which are not taken into account in this table.

nearby countries, especially those operating defined contribution schemes with rates in excess of 20 per cent.

The experience of the SSO in gradually providing coverage to workers in the private sector is presented in Table 3.3.[4] The SSO is also moving to extend coverage to more workers according to its phased plan as described in Section 3.2.1.

The figures in Table 3.3 provide a clear illustration of the impact of the financial crisis, which began in 1997. The number of SSO insured persons declined by 11 per cent in 1998 as compared to 1997. As temporary measures were introduced to reduce contribution rates, in 1998 the SSO scheme's income dropped by 30 per cent, while expenditures increased by 30 per cent. Fortunately, the reserve fund it had built up before the crisis enabled it to cope

---

[4] It is noteworthy that women constitute approximately half of the SSO insurance coverage membership.

Table 3.3: SSO coverage, 1996-1998

	1996	1997	1998
Number of SSO insured persons	5,589,855	6,084,822	5,418,182
As a percentage of private sector employment	51.9	56	54.9
As a percentage of total employment	17.9	19.2	17.6

with this drastic financial situation. Even so, future financial planning by the SSO should take this temporary impact into account.

3.1.2 Other forms of social protection in Thailand

In addition to the contributory Social Security Scheme, the Royal Thai Government offers social protection in the form of public welfare schemes. This includes social assistance, labour protection legislation, government pension and health care schemes for civil servants and voluntary subsidized health cards for people not covered by compulsory health insurance.

The Department of Public Welfare under the aegis of the Ministry of Labour and Social Welfare has a wide range of programmes targeting disadvantaged groups and disaster relief. Services for the elderly include: support for 2,600 elderly persons in 17 residential homes; community support provided through 13 social service centres; and payment of monthly allowances of 300 baht to 400,000 persons. The Department provides vocational training for people with disabilities. It also targets low-income families, including retrenched and unemployed workers receiving no other form of protection. The Department offers financial assistance of up to 4,000 baht per person for a targeted group of 9,000 cases, supported by a total budget of 36 million baht in 1999 (with funding reduced from 1998 when 60 million baht allowed coverage of 15,000 cases); and a credit scheme for the unemployed providing interest-free loans of up to 15,000 baht repayable after five years, intended to promote entrepreneurial initiatives. In the wake of the crisis, the budget for this latter programme increased from 300 million baht in 1998 to 520 million baht in 1999.

The Ministry of Labour and Social Welfare is also responsible for the implementation of the Labour Protection Act, 1998. Significant provisions include the following.

(i)   Severance pay. Under the terms of the 1998 Act, severance entitlements were increased. Depending on length of service the new Act allows for maximum compensation of 10 months' severance pay, compared to the previous maximum of six.

(ii) Employees' Welfare Fund. This was introduced by the 1998 Act, intended to provide compulsory coverage to workers in enterprises with ten or more employees which do not already have an employer-sponsored provident fund. The contribution rate to the Employees' Welfare Fund was initially planned to be set at 10 per cent or less of insurable earnings, shared equally between employers and workers. The accumulated balances in the individual accounts would be available to the worker on separation from employment or death. The Employees' Welfare Fund was meant to complement the Ministry of Finance's 1983 strategy to encourage voluntary retirement benefit schemes.[5] It therefore

---

[5] The Provident Fund Act, 1987 along with the ministerial regulations laid down principles for the structure of these provident fund schemes and their management by private sector companies. As of 1998, there were over 1,000 such provident funds covering over 1 million members.

serves a dual purpose, guaranteeing severance pay and promoting compulsory savings across all sectors of the economy. However, the degree of coordination with other social security provisions is very questionable. At the time of writing the Employees' Welfare Fund was still to be implemented,[6] and the ILO has recommended to the Government that its introduction be postponed indefinitely. This question is explored further in Section 3.2.5.

The Ministry of Labour and Social Welfare also initiated temporary programmes in the wake of the crisis, many of which provided community-based jobs for young people who should have been entering the labour market for the first time.

3.2 Main social protection policy issues

The lack of resources for non-contributory schemes and programmes relying on annual government budget allocations means that developing and expanding the contributory Social Security Scheme constitutes the major policy option for strengthening social protection in Thailand. This section reviews several major policy issues concerning the social protection system.

3.2.1 Extension of social security coverage

Further extensions to the contributory Social Security Scheme are foreseen at various stages. Current plans provide for its extension in 2001 to cover establishments with five to nine workers. According to statistics from the National Statistical Office, this will affect a projected 123,917 establishments employing a total of approximately 1,046,000 workers. In 2005, coverage is expected to extend to workplaces with one to four workers, affecting a projected 1,237,828 establishments employing a total of approximately 3,153,000 workers. In 2007-2016, during the 10th Plan period (2007-2011), feasibility studies are scheduled to examine the possible extension of social protection to the agricultural sector and possible implementation over the following 11th Plan period (2012-2016). In 2017-2021, a special social protection programme covering workers in the fishery and forestry sectors is expected to be planned and implemented.

Undoubtedly, the planned expansion into the agricultural, forestry and fishery sectors will require special consideration and assistance in view of the additional requirements to find ways to adapt the present provisions of the Social Security Act, 1990 to suit the conditions of the rural workforce. It is therefore advisable to pursue what may be a lengthy process of experimentation and planning by studying the feasibility of extending coverage to informal and rural sector workers, possibly focusing mainly on health care and short-term contingencies affecting earnings, such as maternity, in line with the Government's general aim to reach universal health coverage within the next 10-15 years. For example, various groups of home-workers in Thailand, in their efforts to obtain adequate social protection, have built up networks and contacts with NGOs which could help the organization of such administrative arrangements to extend the SSO's coverage.[7] Action to assist home-workers in the field of

---

[6] The Employees' Welfare Fund has not yet been implemented due in the main to questions over timing, and implications for other social protection elements, notably the implementation of the long-term pension schemes in December 1998.

[7] ILO. 1996. *Practical actions for the social protection of home-workers in Thailand* (Bangkok, ILO/ROAP).

social security protection, which would be in accordance with the ILO Home Work Convention, 1996 (No. 177), could establish a conceptual and technical basis for similar initiatives among other groups.

Expanding the contributory Social Security Scheme to reach enterprises with fewer employees presents two main practical difficulties. The SSO's administrative efficiency will be compromised as the average number of insured persons per establishment will be reduced. Today, the average is about 50, but this will fall to less than 30 when enterprises with five to nine employees are covered, and less than ten when enterprises with one to four employees are covered. Secondly, the lower average wage levels in these smaller work units, estimated at 60 to 90 per cent of the overall average in the establishments currently covered, implies some weakening of the revenue flow in respect of the new membership. Meanwhile, the approaches to modifying existing procedures for registering and collecting contributions at smaller enterprises are being reviewed.[8] Yet further labour force coverage is of primary importance to the strengthening of social protection.

3.2.2 Extension of health care

Medical care is a basic and universal need and a key element in social protection systems. Existing provisions in Thailand include four key arrangements.

(i) The public health system provides free medical care to people over 60, low-income persons and their families, the destitute, disabled persons, students, children under the age of 12, veterans and their families and religious leaders – a group which altogether amounts to about 30 million persons. This system was set up in 1975 and coverage expanded as needs have arisen. It is operated under the aegis of the Ministry of Public Health.

(ii) The voluntary health cards scheme caters for between 10 and 12 million persons. This scheme was adopted by the Ministry in 1987 and has been designed to cater for the large population segments falling outside the scope of other public health insurance schemes. Its fundamental aim is to ensure people in the rural and informal sectors have access to comprehensive medical care from a primary care base, operated through a system of low-priced health cards. The cards, which cost only 500 baht, are valid for one year and cover up to five family members. The scheme has gone through various stages and has now attracted a government subsidy of 1000 baht per card. The scheme's 1999 target was to sell about 2.4 million health cards covering 10 million persons.

(iii) The SSO runs compulsory health insurance for about 4.5 million workers.

(iv) The Civil Service Medical Benefits Scheme protects more than 7 million civil servants, retired civil servants receiving pensions and their dependants.

The Health Insurance Office of the Ministry of Public Health recognizes the difficulties of developing an adequate and sustainable national health care scheme as:

(i) despite a 30 day waiting period, the problem of adverse selection (a preponderance of card holders having high expectations of receiving medical care);

---

[8] ILO. 1998a. *Thailand: Review of the social security scheme Part II: Report on health insurance* (Geneva, Social Security Department, ILO/TF/Thailand/R.36 (II)).

(ii)   no control over card purchasers, among whom significant numbers come from outside the target groups, (such as the middle income group including persons who are themselves insured under the Social Security Scheme);[9]

(iii)   hospitals are generally dissatisfied with cost recovery.

Government policies envisage a shift to autonomous self financing health insurance (as under the SSO). Draft legislation has been under discussion for the purposes of designing a scheme for members of the labour force not yet covered by other schemes. Ideally, integrated and coordinated schemes could improve access to adequate, appropriate and affordable health care among various population groups. However, progress has been slow due to difficulties in merging schemes with different financing and benefit principles. Meanwhile, the ILO has provided technical assistance for the reform of the Civil Service Medical Benefits Scheme, which will entail the adoption of the same capitation payment system as social security for out-patient treatment and its reorganization as the Civil Servants' Health Fund. The ILO is also working with the SSO to further develop the compulsory health insurance scheme. The latter offers the most realistic prospects of progress in extending coverage over the next few years.

The Social Security Act, 1990 recognized the importance of organizing improved personal health services for the workforce in the modern sector. Social security health insurance was launched in March 1991 through a national network of contracted public and private hospitals with associated primary care facilities. Providing a full range of medical care for more than 2.7 million insured workers was a considerable undertaking and was feasible only because of the adoption of the capitation provider payment system (which is effective for cost containment and relatively simple to administer), and low utilization rates in the early years.

In the process of extending coverage to close to 5 million workers, the scheme has been developed to ensure improved quality and range of services. Unlike health insurance schemes in many other countries – and the Civil Service Medical Benefits Scheme in Thailand – which have experienced ever-rising costs, in the Social Security Scheme's first five full years, its total expenditure never exceeded 1.25 per cent of insurable earnings. Benefit expenditure as a whole was less than 50 per cent of contribution income. The SSO had thus been willing to provide more resources to extend coverage to non-working spouses and children under the age of six when the emergency cuts were made in contributions. It is estimated that extension to non-working spouses would require the collection of a contribution rate of about 3.2 per cent of insurable earnings (versus 1.25 per cent otherwise) and, if children up to the age of 18 are also included, 4 per cent would be required.[10] This important increase in health protection, which would bring the scheme into conformity with Article Nine of the ILO Social Security (Minimum Standards) Convention, 1951 (No. 102), therefore had to be deferred until the full rates of contributions are again payable in 2001.

The plight of retired workers (including retrenched workers sent on early retirement) must be considered. Their increasing needs for medical care in later life coincide with a decline in incomes, especially as the Social Security Pension Scheme is not designed to pay

---

[9] Persons who are themselves insured under the SSO in many cases have dependents who have not been covered until now.

[10] ILO. 1998b. *Thailand: Review of the social security scheme Part III: Report on the actuarial valuation of short-term benefits* (Geneva, Social Security Department, ILO/TF/Thailand/R36 (III)).

pensions for many years. A health insurance mechanism is needed to ensure continued compulsory coverage as the present arrangement for voluntary membership is open to adverse selection – those in poor health are more likely to perceive the need for health insurance while a limited number are willing to contribute voluntarily. This can be pursued in connection with the development of pensions protection, as discussed in Section 3.2.3.

3.2.3 Strengthening social security pensions

With increasing life expectancy and reduced fertility, persons aged 60 and above now represent more than 8.1 per cent of the population. This will reach 10.2 per cent by 2005 and 13.2 per cent by 2015.[11] SSO statistics show that more than 58 per cent of the insured are under the age of 30 with very low percentages in the highest age groups. The introduction of the social insurance pension scheme was delayed until the end of 1998 due to opposition on cost grounds and differing views on the defined contribution and defined benefits approaches. While the Social Security Scheme represents a significant step forward, there are still some significant gaps that stand between it and the requirements contained in the ILO Social Security (Minimum Standards) Convention, 1951 (No. 102). These differences include:

(i)   the old-age pension income replacement rate for someone who has completed 30 years of insurance is only about 30 per cent of average earnings, which is below the minimum standard specified in the Convention of 40 per cent for a retired worker with a spouse of pensionable age;

(ii) survivors are entitled to lump-sum payments, but not to pensions as specified in the Convention;

(iii) it was stated in the Ministerial Regulations that the pension must not be less than the minimum pension but the SSO has not yet prescribed the exact amount;

(iv) the provisions for invalidity pensions providing an income replacement rate of 50 per cent of earnings are inconsistent with the old-age pension formula;

(v)   there are no transitional provisions for shorter qualifying periods than 180 months to cater for people whose age at the beginning of the scheme meant they had less than 180 months before retirement (usually at the age of 55).

It would be advisable for the SSO to review the scheme urgently to determine how to integrate invalidity benefits and meet the costs of bringing the scheme into conformity with the ILO Convention. As it stands, there are no "grandfathering" provisions allowing transitional rules for awarding old-age pensions. Thus, no pensions will be payable for 15 years (the minimum required for entitlement to a pension) from the starting date. This means that the objective of providing social protection for all will not be achieved for 15 years. Other new schemes in countries similar to Thailand have commonly given older contributors an opportunity to qualify by scaling down the qualifying period required. Partial pensions could be payable after a minimum contribution period of three or five years.

Another important issue is the pensionable age, which has a critical impact on the cost of pension schemes and also tends to influence retirement ages for employees. The age of 55 is relatively low. This could be reviewed in order to examine the many implications of adopting a higher pension age, such as 60 years, with entitlement to early and late retirement. These

---

[11] NESDB. 1995. *Population projections for Thailand, 1990-2020* (Bangkok).

entitlements could be matched with provisions for pension reductions for the former and additional pension rights for the latter. This more flexible approach would better meet the differing personal needs of contributors. Higher standard pension ages would reduce projected costs and therefore increase the feasibility of the proposed changes in key provisions.

Pensioners or retired insured persons should have continuity of coverage for health care, as in nearby countries with both pension and health insurance schemes, e.g. in the Philippines and Viet Nam. In Thailand, retired civil servants and their dependants enjoy health care coverage through the Civil Service Medical Benefits Scheme. The costs of various options for financing this additional benefit for private sector workers should be determined in the scheme revision process proposed above.

Pensions provided under the Workmen's Compensation Fund are of limited duration, as permanent disablement and survivors' pensions are payable for maximum prescribed periods. It is recommended that the legislation be revised on the principle of payment throughout the contingency in accordance with the ILO Social Security (Minimum Standards) Convention, 1951 (No. 102), and the ILO Employment Injury Benefits Convention, 1964 (No. 121).

The policy framework for SSO action on old-age pensions is again under discussion due to the strategies of the fiscal authorities under the Asian Development Bank's Financial Sector Reform Programme. Following the reform of the Government Pension Scheme in 1993 as a combination of defined benefits and defined contributions, a new Government Pension Fund was established in 1997. This increased funds for investment in accordance with the strategy underlying the promotion of company provident funds by the Ministry of Finance through the Provident Fund Act, 1987. The current policy objective is to build-up additional long-term funds for investment by private sector institutions, as is the practice with the existing company provident funds, and thus strengthen capital markets in Thailand. The strategy envisages the reform of the Social Security Pension Scheme and the merging of social security and provident funds into a single system managed by a new institution.

3.2.4 Strengthening occupational safety and health and maternity protection

The Royal Thai Government should pursue its efforts to guarantee a safe working environment for all workers in line with the ILO Programme of Action for Occupational Safety and Health in Thailand towards the Twenty-first Century.[12] Extending the existing maternity protection measures to all women by extending the reach of various social protection measures beyond enterprises of a certain size would also represent a significant step forward.

3.2.5 Introduction of unemployment insurance

Before the economic crisis, Thailand had not accorded any great degree of priority to unemployment insurance. It was specified in the Social Security Act, 1990 without a starting date. In common with most other countries in the region, except China, Mongolia and the Republic of Korea, which have already introduced unemployment insurance, Thailand assumed that these were costly programmes with generally negative effects, especially on labour costs and employment. These views may be based on the contribution rates of 15 per cent appended to the Social Security Act, 1990. There is however, a better appreciation of the positive role and

---

[12] See S. Machida. 1999. *Programme of action for occupational safety and health in Thailand towards the twenty-first century: An advisory report* (Bangkok, ILO/EASMAT).

economic impacts of the schemes now being reviewed in various countries. The benefit concept is that this should provide adequate income support and continued social security coverage for limited periods, without reducing incentives for a prompt return to work. Benefits should also depend on attendance at employment service centres organized to implement active labour market measures. Entitlement to benefits is related not only to contributions, but also to several labour market conditions, taking into account whether unemployment rates are high in the region in which a person lives.

Thailand has begun to consider introducing an unemployment insurance scheme in the wake of the financial crisis, which highlighted the serious limitations of existing mechanisms for providing social protection to retrenched workers. The main statutory rights to social protection are to severance pay and to six months' continued health care coverage under the Social Security Scheme. (According to the SSO, insured persons who were laid off or terminated their employment before December 1999 only will be allowed to extend the free health insurance to 12 months.) Very little data are available on the problems of delayed and unpaid severance compensation, which can cause serious difficulties, especially in periods of recession. The various programmes of the Ministry of Labour and Social Welfare and other government agencies have helped to alleviate some of the worst effects of unemployment. Even so, the limitations of ad hoc measures and of schemes relying on government budget appropriations only serve to underline the need for a well-designed and feasible unemployment insurance scheme.

At the request of the Government, the ILO conducted a study in 1998 to examine the financial and administrative feasibility of unemployment insurance.[13] In order to provide policy options, cost projections were made for the period from 2001 to 2007 for three standards of benefit based on a number of assumptions regarding the macro-economic and labour market framework. According to this study, the earliest feasible starting date is 2001. There are three options:

(i)   Option 1: Benefits of 50 per cent of average earnings for a maximum period of three months, subject to a qualifying period of six months' insurance out of the last 15 months prior to unemployment;

(ii)   Option 2: Benefits of 50 per cent of average earnings for a maximum period of six months if contributions are paid for at least ten months in the 15 months ending three months before the unemployment;

(iii)   Option 3: Same as option 2, except that claimants over the age of 50 with 20 months' insurance out of the last 30 months ending three months preceding the claim would be entitled to benefit for up to 12 months.

Table 3.4 provides the estimated contribution rates, as a percentage of insurable earnings, that would be required to establish and maintain an unemployment insurance scheme. These estimates cover not only the benefit expenditure but also the costs of administration. They also cover the cost of building up and maintaining a contingency reserve representing 12 months of projected benefit expenditure.

---

[13] See ILO. 1998c. *Thailand: Assessment of the feasibility of introducing an unemployment insurance scheme in Thailand, Report to the Government* (Geneva, Social Security Department).

Table 3.4: Unemployment insurance: Estimated contribution rates on the basis of implementation effective in 2001

(As a percentage of insurable earnings)

Year	Option 1	Option 2	Option 3
2001	2.5	2.5	2.6
2002	1.2	1.6	1.7
2003	0.9	1.3	1.3
2004	0.7	1.1	1.1
2005	0.6	0.8	0.9
2006	0.4	0.6	0.6
2007 +	0.4	0.6	0.6

Source: ILO. 1998c. *Thailand: Assessment of the feasibility of introducing an unemployment insurance scheme in Thailand,* Report to the Government (Bangkok, Social Security Department, ILO, Geneva and ILO/EASMAT).

The ILO study indicates that the proposed scheme would have minimal effects on aggregate disposable income, consumption, savings and individual purchasing power, or on aggregate consumption, labour costs and the aggregate consumer price levels. It also stresses that not having such a scheme involves economic costs, including worker opposition to structural changes and new technologies.

Basic operating requirements include a considerable expansion of the network of employment services offices, attainment of satisfactory operating standards from the new SSO on-line computer system and collaboration between SSO and the employment services in the running of the scheme. The report advises that a decision to introduce unemployment insurance in principle would need to be made at an early stage to facilitate the preparations for its launch. ILO estimates made in mid-1998 were premised on a target date in 2001. A Ministry of Labour and Social Welfare working group is studying this and related questions. In the event that unemployment insurance is adopted and implemented, the introduction of the proposed Employees' Welfare Fund may be postponed indefinitely.

Unemployment insurance appears to be a major priority in the context of the development of a global social protection policy in Thailand. Its administration could take place more easily through close collaboration between the SSO and employment services. Even if we work on the assumption that the SSO might ultimately be responsible for implementing unemployment insurance, it is imperative that this is integrated with employment services. It is particularly important that there is timely reporting of new hires to the administration of the unemployment insurance scheme. In any case, a substantial increase in employment services staff levels would be necessary for the operation of an unemployment insurance scheme.

3.3 Major recommendations

3.3.1 Establishing a social protection coordination committee or commission

There is no institutional mechanism specifically designed to oversee policy formulation and coordination over the entire field of social protection. Wider acceptance of the importance of social protection and of the need to prepare for economic downturns has meant that policy coordination has become more important than ever. A social protection coordination committee or commission could improve policy cohesion and coordination.

There are several major issues which a coordinating commission or committee might examine. Some of these are within the scope of social security and the Ministry of Labour and Social Welfare, while others concern national health and fiscal policies. There are policy issues to be resolved between the partially funded social insurance pension approach adopted by the SSO and the Ministry of Finance strategy of integrating fully funded pension and provident funds into one system under an institution linked to private sector fund management. The defined benefit principle and partial funding system would seem to be the most appropriate forms for the pension scheme to be implemented by the SSO. While this particular problem might be considered on an urgent basis by the proposed social security committee, in which all interests are represented, the overall coordinating authority might be vested in the Ministry of Labour and Social Welfare in view of its extensive responsibilities for social protection, as previously suggested by the ILO,[14] with the collaboration of the Ministry of Finance and the Ministry of Public Health as a minimum requirement.

The commission or committee might also usefully examine the financing of social assistance benefits, which are administered by the Ministry of Labour and Social Welfare using budget allocations from the Ministry of Finance. As is the case in most countries, there are difficulties with targeting and means-testing social assistance. However, Thailand's village assistance centres could help with these tasks if extra funding could be found to expand the scheme, together with targeted capacity building. The resource limitations cannot be fully overcome in the short term, but on grounds of equity there is a case for considering a phased development of improved scales of assistance, at least for the elderly in rural households. The considerable financial support provided by the Government under the Social Security Act, 1990 for persons in employment and for the Voluntary Health Care Scheme adds weight to this argument. The proposed committee or commission (or the Ministry of Labour and Social Welfare and the Ministry of Finance) might consider additional funding for social assistance as part of an overall review of social assistance policies. A policy to advocate and enforce maternity protection should also be included.

3.3.2 Introduction of unemployment insurance

The 1998 ILO study assessing the introduction of unemployment insurance in Thailand[15] pointed out that unemployment insurance can be introduced only by 2001, even provided that the decision-making and administrative process was initiated in 1998. While there are obvious differences of opinion among social partners on the timing of the scheme, the Government might wish to consider making a decision in principle to introduce unemployment insurance and issue a Royal Decree as early as possible. The government might also consider undertaking a thorough examination of the policy and organization of employment services to support unemployment insurance, especially their administrative infrastructure and integration with unemployment insurance. The unemployment insurance system should only be put in place if integrated with employment services for the two key purposes of reporting and training for

---

[14] ILO. 1995. *Thailand: Pensions and family benefits*, Report to the Government of Thailand on the development of social protection, (Bangkok, ILO and ILO/EASMAT, Social Security Department).

[15] See ILO. 1998c.

skills upgrading.[16] This would also involve developing special measures to account for the existence of private employment services.

The ILO estimated the cost of unemployment insurance in the long-term at approximately 0.5 per cent of insurable earnings, with a higher cost at the outset to meet the initial expenses of setting up the scheme. This is considered reasonable given the current stage of economic development in Thailand.

3.3.3 Development priorities of the Social Security Office

The SSO might consider setting up a medium-term development plan to establish clear strategic objectives and work plans in respect of the following:

(i)   extension of coverage to workers of small-size enterprises (five to nine workers);

(ii) extension of coverage to workers of micro-enterprises (one to four workers) and to the rural and informal sectors, including the possibility to work through micro-insurance schemes and providing support through community-based schemes;

(iii) assessment of the possible extension of health care coverage to non-working spouses, children under the age of 18 years and retired members of the SSO;

(iv) studying measures to improve pensions provisions for old-age and workmen's compensation with particular reference to relevant ILO standards and mechanisms;

(v)   the preparation of unemployment insurance;

(vi) a measure to ensure the regular adjustment of the upper limit on insurable earnings to account for inflation. In parallel, adjustment measures should be reflected on the level of benefits in payment.

3.3.4 Strengthening the Social Security Office

The SSO is confronted with the challenging task of developing and implementing a comprehensive and efficient social protection system in Thailand. It has accomplished much in its short existence. Even so, it faces considerable challenges in meeting the growing need for social protection among all sections of the workforce. The Ministry of Labour and Social Welfare has provided leadership and guidance through the very difficult early years and the tripartite Social Security Committee, with the assistance of the Medical Committee, has played a key role. The SSO, however, is subject to severe staffing constraints imposed by the Civil Service Commission, and now functions with only 1,944 civil servants, 441 permanent employees and 2,225 temporary staff. The government budget pays for the civil servants and permanent employees, while the costs of the temporary staff are met through the SSO's administrative budget. Budget constraints are the underlying reason why the SSO can lack control over its personnel and have to rely heavily on temporary staff for its operational activities.

---

[16] As an unemployment insurance scheme provides temporary assistance to retrenched workers, it must be integrated with training programmes for their reintroduction into the work force. These are usually provided through employment services whether sponsored by the government, private initiatives or at the enterprise level. The unemployment insurance is thus a temporary measure assisting in the process of turnover of workers from one employer to another.

It is, of course, most desirable that the SSO acquire in-house expertise and experience and build up a sizeable cadre of professional social security administrators. In order to prevent the loss of experienced and capable staff through transfers under civil service rules, the SSO should become an independent and autonomous agency under the auspices of the Ministry of Labour and Social Welfare. This model of an autonomous body under tripartite supervision and answerable to the competent ministry, which is accountable to Parliament, is widely used in the social security field. It offers technical advantages and is an area of significant importance for the social partners and for the progress of social and economic development. Conditions of service in the new agency might be made more attractive than those on offer in the civil service to help the agency recruit and retain qualified staff.

Chapter 4

Skills development for growth, productivity and long-term competitiveness

4.1 Skills as a constraint on competitiveness

The relatively low education and skill levels of the Thai workforce will be one of the key factors influencing Thailand's international competitiveness as it faces increasing pressure from the effects of globalization and liberalization. More than 70 per cent of the workforce has only a primary school or lower education level. This lack of appropriate skills was a key finding of a 1997 Foreign Investors Confidence Survey conducted by the Office of the Board of Investment. The survey found that investors saw shortages of skilled labour as a more serious constraint to investing in Thailand than either bureaucratic inertia or inadequate infrastructure.[1] Moreover, the recent financial crisis has shown that the benefits of involvement in global markets can accrue on a sustainable basis only if the country has a well-educated labour force that can adapt its skills quickly in response to the changing demands of the global market place.

The Thai education and training system has several structural weaknesses. Although up to 12 line ministries conduct a wide variety of skill training programmes, only a small percentage of the present workforce has received any systematic training. Many years of high growth do not seem to have contributed a great deal to improving the education and skill levels of workers. The education and training system has not been able to produce enough qualified workers to cope with the increasing demand and thereby support the transition to high-technology industries.

Despite persistent Government efforts to improve and upgrade the education and training systems, in many areas Thailand still lags behind its East Asian neighbours. Technology and industry policies, which logically should go hand-in-hand with HRD policies, have often either not been articulated or have not been analysed for HRD needs. This has created constraints on economic performance due to a lack of flexibility in the labour force and a skill profile of limited relevance to opportunities offered by global markets.

The availability of highly skilled, adaptable workers is crucial to ensure efficient and productive enterprises and to achieve higher productivity levels and competitiveness within the economy. New technologies and new forms of work organization induce higher productivity. New skills are required to handle new technologies and to set up and operate new forms of work organization and modern production systems. In many cases, this involves a different attitude to work, new definitions of occupational categories and new management systems, all of which require the constant upgrading of skills. The new forms of work organization will bring about a shift away from the traditional, hierarchical, command-and-control approaches to more flexible teamwork to organize well-defined routines and clearly demarcated tasks. This will require a much more flexible and responsive public training system and a greatly increased role for enterprises as training providers.

---

[1] World Bank, Thailand and the ONEC. 1999. *Secondary and vocational education in Thailand, moving towards 12 years for all: A study of policy options* (Bangkok).

The industrial sector carries out a considerable amount of skills training to overcome skills shortages. However, enterprise training has limitations. Many large firms and most small firms limit their employee training to meeting operational needs rather than looking to technological upgrading and retraining of workers in line with new technologies [Middleton and Tzannatos, 1998]. A recent World Bank study[2] reports, however, that large firms not only attract and keep high-level staff by paying them higher wages than small firms, but also provide them with more training. The study goes on to suggest that the inability of small firms to match the wages of larger firms, and the constraints on providing additional training, are the main reasons why they lack skilled workers. The pattern of in-plant training is not conducive to export competitiveness, or increasing local content or technological deepening [Lall, 1999]. While this pattern is common to many countries because of numerous market failures in enterprise training, it holds back productivity and the introduction of new technologies. Training has been shown to be positively associated with firm-level productivity in five countries in a World Bank study.[3]

4.2 Human resources development and training – the present situation

4.2.1 The present skills situation

According to Zeufack (1999), low qualifications, and not unemployment, were the main concern relating to the Thai labour market between 1986 and 1996. They might remain the most serious threat to increasing labour productivity and regaining competitiveness after the financial crisis of July 1997. Unlike most countries in East Asia, the manufacturing sector was essentially based on low-qualification labour-intensive industries in 1996, according to this study. Only 5 per cent of workers hired by firms had been to college or university. Around 10 per cent had completed upper secondary school and 22 per cent had lower secondary level education. Some 11 per cent had attended vocational training schools and around 53 per cent had primary level education or less. Compared with local firms, foreign firms employed twice as many college/university level staff and had more than twice as many staff with upper secondary level education.

A report by the Thailand Development Research Institute (TDRI)[4] suggests that most small and medium-sized industries are still using low technology and require cheap labour to be competitive. Large firms use imported technology but current labour force skills are only adequate for operating and maintaining these technologies. Consequently, the skills required for a shift to higher value-added and higher technology industries are in very short supply. Thailand has only 15 engineers/scientists per 10,000 of the population. In 1995, the deficit of qualified workers was so acute that, despite the inadequate quality standards of the vocational training institutes, the placement rate of its graduates reached 90 per cent against 50 per cent in the mid 1980s.[5] It is expected that by 2001, there will be a substantial shortfall in the supply of engineers and scientists at the degree level, even at the current levels of demand. The

---

[2] Albert G. Zeufack. 1999. *Employer-provided training under oligopolistic labour markets* (Washington D.C., World Bank).

[3] Tan Hong; Batra Geeta. 1995. *Enterprise training in developing countries: Incidence, productivity effects and policy implications* (Washington D.C., World Bank).

[4] TDRI. 1998. *Human resource development plan for Thailand's manufacturing and service industry 1997-2006*, Report prepared for the DSD, (Bangkok, TDRI (unofficial English translation by ILO/EASMAT)).

[5] Albert G. Zeufack. op. cit.

situation will be far worse if industry shifts to more skill-intensive technology. Table 4.1 shows the projected shortfall. To overcome this problem, the Government will need to develop a range of incentives and programmes to encourage young people and, in particular, young women, to study mathematics and science at secondary school. This would enable a much greater number of people to study engineering and science at university level. Table 4.2 reveals the relatively low number of students studying these subjects compared to the social sciences.

4.2.2 The education and training system

(a) The education system

Thailand allocates a high percentage of its national budget to education and training. For example, spending on education reached 22 per cent of public expenditure in 1997. However, educational achievements lag far behind other newly industrialized countries. The education system is coming under close scrutiny as the country tries to provide the higher skills base needed to increase competitiveness and achieve higher value-added production.

Table 4.1: Thailand: Estimated science and technology manpower gaps at current level of demand

(Number of persons)

Field of study	Planned output		Incremental		Manpower gap	
	1996	2001	1996	2001	1996	2001
B. Engineering	13,066	17,156	16,294	26,437	4,520	10,963
B. Science	4,938	8,506	9,329	12,970	5,874	7,015
M. Eng/D. Eng.	676	949	856	1,490	180	541
MS/DS	874	1,338	761	986	–113	–352

Source: The Brooker Group. 1997. BOI Vision Support Doc. (Bangkok).

Table 4.2: University students in 1997 (ISCED classification)

No.	Branch	Number			Per cent of women
		Women	Men	Total	
1.	Humanities	17,368	4,672	22,040	73.8
2.	Medicine and related areas	49,748	14,484	55,333	73.82
3.	Social science	224,324	161,229	385,553	58.18
4.	Education	32,900	24,082	56,982	57.74
5.	Natural science	22,229	21,878	44,107	50.4
6.	Fine arts and applied arts	1,481	1,838	3,319	44.62
7.	Agriculture, forestry and fisheries	11,249	15,311	26,560	42.35
8.	Law	21,520	85,289	106,809	20.15
9.	Engineering and architecture	7,147	38,376	45,523	15.7
10.	Others	1,667	1,629	3,296	50.58
	Total	380,734	368,788	749,522	50.8

Source: State University Bureau, cited in: N. Theeravit. June 1999. *Toward Gender Equality at Work in Thailand,* paper prepared for ILO/EASMAT (Bangkok).

There has been impressive progress in expanding primary education in Thailand, but in the secondary and tertiary sectors matters are less satisfactory. Middleton and Tzannatos[6] report that many of the resources available at upper secondary level are devoted to expensive vocational education. These schools enrol 45 per cent of the upper secondary students and provide pre-employment training that was appropriate for the early stages of Thailand's industrialization but is increasingly inappropriate for the present economy. At the tertiary level, the concerns are mainly to do with outdated curricula, lack of practical training, the lack of contact with the evolving needs of industry and the low qualifications of many of the university faculty (approximately half have less than a Master's degree).[7] A further underlying constraint on improving the skills of the present workforce is the low functional literacy rate of Thai workers. Functional literacy, using the United Nations Educational, Scientific and Cultural Organization (UNESCO) definition, means the level of literacy or numeracy required to solve problems that are new and unrelated to previous experience. It is generally considered that around six years of formal education are needed to achieve functional literacy.[8] While the figures in Table 4.3 show a substantial improvement in functional literacy rates for the target population (14-59 years), and imply a continuous improvement, the rates drop sharply for people 30 years of age and older. As these people are beyond the reach of the school system, achieving further improvement will require the development of special adult literacy and numeracy programmes in the workplace.

Table 4.3: Functional literacy rates by age groups

(Percentages)

Age groups	1992	1997	Change
12 to 14 years	69.9	60.4	-9.6
15 to 17 years	93.5	95.7	2.2
18 to 24 years	86.1	92.0	5.9
25 to 29 years	53.9	82.5	28.7
30 to 39 years	31.5	46.4	14.9
40 to 49 years	17.7	23.5	5.8
50 to 59 years	9.6	14.7	5.1
All age groups	51.9	57.3	5.4

Source: Children and Youth Survey, NSO, processed by Development Evaluation Division, NESDB.

The 1997 Constitution provides the foundation for reforming the education system by giving all citizens the right to 12 years of publicly financed education. The new Education Act, passed in August 1999, provides the legal framework. Funding constraints and bureaucratic inertia may, however, delay the introduction of the 12 year standard. Current secondary

---

[6] J. Middleton and Z. Tzannatos. 1998. *Skills for competitiveness* in, NESDB/World Bank: *Competitiveness and sustainable economic recovery in Thailand*, Vol. 2, Background papers for the Conference on Thailand's Dynamic Economic Recovery and Competitiveness (Bangkok, NESDB and the World Bank Thailand Office).

[7] S. Lall. 1999. *Raising competitiveness in the Thai economy*, op. cit.

[8] NESDB. 1999. *Indicators of well-being and policy analysis*, in *NESDB Newsletter*, Vol. 3, No. 2 (Bangkok).

enrolment stands at only 30 per cent of the eligible age group and 80 per cent of the total population did not attend secondary school. In addition, there is now a higher dropout rate as a result of the economic slump. A detailed profile of the gross and net enrolment rates is shown in Table 4.4. The gross enrolment rate is the percentage of the population in the relevant age group for a particular level – it reflects the absorptive capacity of the system, not its coverage. The net enrolment rates, alternatively, show the number of students enrolled in a level of education who belong to the relevant age group as the percentage of the population in that age group. The misplacement index is the difference between the gross and net enrolment rates and reflects the percentage of students who are either under- or over-aged for their education levels. While the gross enrolment rates show an impressive improvement over the five-year period shown, the net enrolment rates show a more modest improvement with only 55 and 24 per cent in the lower and upper secondary levels respectively. A considerable amount of work still needs to be done if the educational objectives of the Eighth Plan are to be achieved.[9] It is now generally agreed that strengthening general education, in particular at the primary and secondary levels, should be a key priority in public policies to improve the productivity and flexibility of the workforce. The general education level is closely linked to human resources development in general, and the "trainability" of the potential workforce, i.e. the ease with which people can be trained.

The primary and secondary education systems will also need to change to support the development of a flexible workforce. In Thailand, the system of education is very much a "passive" learning environment. A "learning-to-learn" approach needs to become more widespread, with students researching their own information and learning to work in teams. At the secondary school level there should be greater efforts to expose students to the world of work, using systems such as the school-to-work programme.

Table 4.4: Gross and net enrolment rates and educational misplacement index: Whole Kingdom

Level	Gross enrolment rate	Net enrolment rate	Per cent of younger children in level	Per cent of children	Misplacement index
1992					
Pre-school	38.1	14.4	0.0	23.6	23.6
Primary	100.1	77.0	0.1	23.1	23.2
Lower secondary	59.3	36.5	0.8	22.0	22.8
Upper secondary	20.1	13.8	0.5	5.9	6.3
Higher education	11.3	8.5	2.8	0.0	2.8
1997					
Pre-school	61.1	35.7	0.0	25.4	25.4
Primary	105.8	84.8	0.1	21.0	21.1
Lower secondary	91.7	55.1	0.5	36.1	36.5
Upper secondary	36.2	24.0	0.2	11.9	12.1
Higher education	20.6	15.1	5.5	0.0	5.5

Source: Children and Youth Survey, NSO, processed by Development Evaluation Division, NESDB.

---

[9] NESDB. 1999. *Indicators of well-being and policy analysis*, op. cit.

(b)   The technical and vocational education and vocational training systems

Thailand has long recognized the importance of good technical and vocational education (TVE), and vocational training (VT) practices. Responsibility is spread across several ministries and there is an impressive network of training institutions, in both the public and the private sectors. Large numbers of people are involved in the planning, implementation, control and monitoring of the system and subsystems. The subject is of high priority at the highest levels of Government, with the Cabinet Committee on Economic Policy receiving regular briefings on the vocational training activities and achievements of the Ministry of Labour and Social Welfare to mitigate against the social impact of the financial situation. Thus, most of the ingredients are there for good systems, i.e. top level· involvement and commitment, widespread coverage and facilities, financial allocation and assigned staff.

The principal institution delivering VT in Thailand is the Ministry of Labour and Social Welfare, through its Department of Skill Development (DSD); together with the private sector, through on-the-job enterprise training and private training providers. The principal institution delivering TVE is the Ministry of Education, through its departments of Vocational Education and Non-formal Education.

However, there is a lack of national coordination of the various elements and means of delivery within the system. Each part seems to have total autonomy over what it can and should do, irrespective of whether its actions duplicate or negate the activities of other parts. While there is considerable emphasis on HRD in the Eighth Plan, there is a lack of clear-cut policy in the TVE and VT sectors. There is also a lack of effective linkages between employment and public providers, with the possible exception of the Ministry of Industry and the Ministry of Labour and Social Welfare, where training needs for small-scale industry development are analysed by the former and provided for by the latter. However, even in this case, training for entrepreneurship and self-employment is not well developed. Another area of weakness, critically important for national and enterprise competitiveness, is the lack of linkage between TVE and VT, productivity and the utilization of new technology. With some notable exceptions, which are explained in the following section, industry has very little involvement in the design and development of public sector courses.

Many countries in Asia are experiencing difficulties in coordinating their systems of technical and vocational education with those of vocational training – these difficulties are not unique to Thailand. The problems are similar and usually stem from the same root cause of many agencies providing similar courses, often for the same target groups, leading to a waste of scarce resources and a duplication of efforts. The lack of clear definitions of target groups and uncertainty over the delineation of responsibility between providers and their comparative advantages is rarely addressed. Each training institution awards its own certificates, which can tend to lower standards and confuse employers. In many countries in Asia and the Pacific there are several line ministries conducting pre-employment vocational education courses and a number of other ministries conducting a range of sector-specific VT courses for their own employees. Employers find it difficult to interact with the training system at the national and regional levels.

The responsibility for coordination of TVE and VT in Thailand is divided between two agencies. TVE comes under the National Education Commission, while VT comes under the National Vocational Training Coordination Committee (NVTCC). The Commission plays a major role in policy development and monitoring for all forms of education; the NVTCC is only concerned with vocational training. The Department of Skill Development, through the Ministry of Labour and Social Welfare, acts as the secretariat of the NVTCC which is chaired by the Prime Minister.

In 1997, the Ministry of Labour and Social Welfare signed agreements with eight other line ministries to cooperate in skills training, namely the Ministry of Defence, the Ministry of Science Technology and Environment, the Ministry of Education, the Ministry of the Interior, the Ministry of Industry, the Ministry of Transport and Communication, the Ministry of University Affairs and the Tourism Authority of Thailand, along with the Bangkok Metropolitan Authority and other private sector organizations. Under the NVTCC there are two groups of subcommittees: provincial vocational training coordination subcommittees to promote effective and systematic labour development and vocational training at the local level, and the Human Resource Master Plan Development Subcommittee to ensure uniformity of development and growth distribution to the provincial level. This subcommittee was set up to study labour market information, prepare short- and long-term human resource development plans and submit them to NVTCC for consideration.

The NVTCC commissioned the Human Resource Development Master Plan for the Manufacturing and Service Sectors for Thailand (2000-2006) mentioned earlier [TDRI, 1998]. The master plan sets the targets for manpower production in education and training according to the needs of all manufacturing sectors in Thailand.

The NVTCC has faced considerable difficulty in performing its stated tasks, the major constraint being that it rarely meets. It also suffers from many alterations to its composition as the governing coalition changes, bringing corresponding ministerial changes as it does. If it can overcome some of these obstacles, perhaps become tripartite in nature and work with a strengthened and expanded secretariat, the NVTCC does offer some hope as a national coordinating mechanism, the status of which is enhanced through being chaired by the Prime Minister.

4.2.3 The vocational training delivery system and observed problems

(a) The Department of Skill Development (Ministry of Labour and Social Welfare)

The DSD has a national network of training centres and institutions providing pre-employment training for school dropouts, upgrading training to develop the skills of existing workers, non-agricultural training for people in the rural areas and a range of specific training courses based on requests from enterprises. The DSD's work is based on tripartite principles and its mandate includes providing training in response to labour market needs and providing skills for the disadvantaged so that their chances of obtaining employment are improved. The DSD operates an Occupational Skill Standards System through a subcommittee composed of representatives of the public and private sectors. The DSD is presently revising the 41 existing standards and developing 43 new standards, using a form of competency-based training, with the assistance of the Asian Development Bank. The DSD also administers the Skills Development Fund, a loan scheme which supports skills development. The Fund had a total of 300 million baht available and, as of 26 May 1999, loans totalling 298.8 million baht had been granted.

The DSD also manages a range of incentives to encourage enterprises to organize training for workers, under the Vocational Training Promotion Act, 1994. The main purpose of the Act is to support vocational training for workers to help them develop the skills required by Thai industry. The Act is also intended to promote cooperation between the public training system and private enterprises. The DSD is in the process of revising the Act with a view to attracting more enterprises to the scheme. This revision, called the Skill Development Promotion Bill will add a provision on the Skill Development Fund and will offer more coverage and more benefits to enterprises. Some of the revised provisions include the following.

(i)   Encouraging enterprises to set up skills training centres. Apart from an additional 50 per cent allowance for tax reduction equivalent to the cost of the training expenses, the enterprises will receive exemption from import duty for machinery and training equipment as well as additional 50 per cent allowances for power and water bills. They can also bring in foreigners as training instructors.

(ii)   Promoting the use of occupational skills standard testing by the private sector, allowing the firm, association or educational institution to set up an occupational skills standard testing centre.

For small and medium-sized enterprises, the DSD provides assistance in developing training curricula, purchasing training equipment and developing instructors within the enterprises. The enterprises are entitled to register as training providers under the revised Act with the Department acting as a mentor.

In order to assist workers laid off as a result of the slow down of the economy due to the financial crisis, the DSD has organized a number of retraining programmes funded by the World Bank, the Asian Development Bank and the Miyazawa Fund.

These programmes have resulted in a dramatic increase in the overall numbers trained by the DSD. While in 1997 the total number of people trained, in all courses, was around 420,000, the target for training in 1998 was expected to be as high as 650,000 persons.[10]

However, the DSD is facing several challenges. As part of the national training system, it suffers from the lack of effective coordination referred to above, resulting in a duplication of efforts with other bodies carrying out training programmes. The occupational skills standards and the associated trade standards testing are in need of substantial revision as, at present, it is considered that they do not meet the needs of the labour market for workers or employers. The existing standards, however, are presently being revised. As most of the trainees in the pre-employment courses come from a weak formal education system, the quality of entry-level trainees is not high. It is difficult to see how school dropouts can be turned into highly skilled workers in courses lasting less than one year. While the Department has made substantial progress in promoting training in the private sector, it will need to expanded considerably if the enterprises are to share adequately the adult training load. The DSD is presently being assisted to expand and develop its programmes through an US$ 80 million loan from the Asian Development Bank.

(b)   Training in enterprises

Zeufack (1999) provides important data on training in enterprises.[11] His study was based on the Thai Industrial and Competitiveness Survey conducted between the last quarter of 1997

---

[10] Areeya Rojvithee. 1999. *Successful practices in HRD in the workplace: Contributions from labour, management and government, case studies from Thailand*, (Bangkok, DSD, MOLSW, unpublished).

[11] Albert G. Zeufack. 1999. op. cit.

and the first quarter of 1998 and covered 1200 plants in five industries. It represents the first attempt to assess the extent and the intensity of employer-provided training in Thailand. According to Zeufack:

The results of the study are unequivocal. Workers and firms have relied heavily on "on-the-job" training to respond to the skill needs of a rapidly growing economy that set technological upgrading of the industrial base as one of its targets in 1993. Indeed, firms do train extensively in Thailand; 88 per cent of firms in the sample provide training of some kind to employees, 82 per cent give informal training to new workers and 58 per cent provide formal training to employees.

This study provides a picture of training in enterprises that differs from an earlier 1991 study by Middleton et al.,[12] which concluded that a large share of small and medium-sized firms, together with some large firms, fail to provide training because of the low education levels of workers.

Over the past 15 years or so, small firms have become increasingly important to national and regional economies and have strongly influenced competitiveness, working conditions and living standards. But research in several countries has shown that there is a systematic tendency towards a lower provision of formal training in smaller firms, especially among the very smallest. The Zeufack study has confirmed this trend in the case of Thailand. This is because larger firms are more certain of reaping the full private benefit of their training expenditures than are smaller firms. In the case of very small firms, there is also a strong argument that training institutions do not attempt to reach out to such firms and offer the kind of training needed, with flexible timing and instruction related to the educational levels of the potential trainees. In the informal sector, this is of particular importance to women.

A major trend which has been recognized through the analysis of the operation of small and medium-sized companies is that the competitive capabilities of individual small firms and their accompanying incomes and working conditions, are crucially affected by the quality of inter-firm and firm-institution networks in which the small firm is embedded. Consequently, much policy attention is now focused on addressing the needs of whole groups, networks or sectoral clusters of firms, rather than dealing with enterprises solely on an individual basis.

Further, an accompanying trend is the increased attention being paid to issues of knowledge acquisition and dissemination as crucial components of competitiveness. This is the case with Thailand trying to catch up with more advanced countries and, indeed, with highly industrialized countries trying to move their economies along higher value-adding paths of development. An interesting development in some other countries has been the use of innovative new programmes and initiatives to address the associated issues of training, learning and knowledge transfer in the context of promoting small firms as part of inter-firm and firm-institution networks.[13] Three specific types of inter-firm networks could be appropriate for Thailand: business networks, commodity chains and sectoral clusters.

---

[12] J. Middleton; P. Nipon; R. Omporn; S. Chantavit. 1991. *Vocational training in a changing economy – the case of Thailand,* (Washington D.C., World Bank, working paper).

[13] Middleton; P. Nipon; R. Omporn; S. Chantavit. op. cit.

The main public sector providers have been making considerable efforts to promote training within enterprises. The Dual Vocational Training Project in the Department of Vocational Education (DOVE) is currently targeting 50 companies in which training will be provided as part of the dual system of vocational training. The project would ultimately like to target 2,900 companies for inclusion in the dual system approach. As noted earlier, the DSD also manages a range of programmes to encourage private sector enterprises to take in unemployed people and train them in various skills. The tax incentive scheme, for example, takes the form of allowances for tax reduction equivalent to the cost of the training expenses. DSD implementation statistics up to September 1999 show that 624 enterprises have taken part in the scheme, providing 5,430 training courses (all approved by the DSD) for a total of 460,407 workers at a total cost of 656.6 million baht. The Vocational Training Promotion Act, 1994 also allows private sector firms to register as training providers, for which they are entitled to a 50 per cent deduction in their income tax for training expenses. By September 1999, there were 40 registered providers under this scheme. There is also a scheme to promote the establishment of private training institutes through loans provided by the Government Savings Bank. There are currently 20 companies registered under this scheme. The DSD has also approved the establishment of 12 skill testing places for overseas workers and of 24,779 workers tested in 1999, 20,478 passed. There were also ten skill testing centres created and of 5,518 workers tested, 4,086 passed. The DSD also trained 7,034 people, of which 2,936 were women, at the request of a number of enterprises. The reasons for the relatively low participation rates in these various schemes is not clear, given that a large number of Thai firms seem to provide some form of training for their workers. A detailed study and review of the effectiveness of these schemes is a priority. This issue will be taken up in the final section dealing with policy options.

4.2.4 The technical and vocational education delivery system and observed problems

(a) The Department of Vocational Education and Non-Formal Education (Ministry of Education)

The Department of Vocational Education has wide national coverage of vocational education, with an impressive network of vocational education institutions. There is an active donor programme, with an ongoing Dual Vocational Training Project introducing the dual system methodology for apprenticeship training. A new Vocational Education and Training Act is in the process of being drafted for approval. Follow-up tracer studies are carried out on all trainees six months after they complete their training. Table 4.5 shows the employment situation of the 1996 graduates of the formal programme. Of the total of 68,626 graduates who responded to the survey, 46,224 (67 per cent) had gone on to further study. Some 18,841 (28 per cent) were employed and 2,643 (4 per cent) were unemployed.

The Department of Non-Formal Education also provides a wide range of adult community training programmes for school leavers and adults. One of its main programmes is adult equivalent general education programmes at the primary, lower and upper secondary levels. In 1998, there were approximately 60,000 participants in this programme.

In the DOVE system, however, there are a number of emerging weaknesses. As Table 4.5 indicates, most programmes serve as bridges to higher courses instead of focusing on employment opportunities or producing skilled workers for industry; such bridges tend to be a very expensive means of moving students to further or higher education. Vocational education

Table 4.5: Employment status of graduates (formal programme), academic year 1995, work entry 1996

Employment summary	A	B	C	D	Total
Total graduates	59,412	1,611	30,859	516	92,398
Number of responses	45,304	1,182	21,750	390	68,626
Further study	38,129	410	7,677	8	46,224
Employed	5,836	627	12,009	369	18,841
– *Government*	*295*	*36*	*759*	*211*	*1,301*
– *Private*	*4,597*	*548*	*10,404*	*156*	*15,705*
– *Self*	*944*	*43*	*846*	*2*	*1,835*
Unemployed	911	112	1,528	12	2,643
– *Waiting*	*413*	*55*	*813*	*10*	*1,291*
– *Rejected*	*578*	*57*	*715*	*2*	*1,352*
Others	348	33	536	1	918

Source: DOVE: *Statistics 1997*, Ministry of Education.

Legend:
A = Certificate in Vocational Education (Cert. Voc.)
B = Diploma in Technician Education (Dip. Tech.)
C = Diploma in Vocational Education (Dip. Voc.)
D = Higher Diploma in Technical Education (High Dip. Voc.)

and training is not linked very closely to workplace productivity. There are limited vocational guidance, counselling and placement services available. There is no effective coordination of DOVE services with other vocational education and training providers and existing national occupational skill standards have no linkages with the DOVE curricula, making it difficult to have an effective skill recognition system. A further problem is that 50 per cent of applicants for training places are rejected, raising questions about the efficiency of the use of facilities and resources. The low levels of basic education tend to limit the achievements of trainees and overall skill levels are low. The DOVE network of vocational education institutions does have the potential, though, to provide the longer-term training required to produce the highly-skilled workers of the future. This point is discussed further in section 4.5.2.

4.3 Training for specific groups

(a) The special needs of women across all target groups

While the lack of access to education and exclusion from workplace-based training is one of the main forms of discrimination against women in many countries of the region, the picture in Thailand is not clear. The enrolment figures for general education show very little variation between males and females (see Table 4.6). However, according to an ILO/Asian Institute of Technology (AIT) study,[14] the proportion of women to men among those with higher education is one woman to two men.

---

[14] ILO/AIT. 1998. *Gender, policy and the economic crisis*, Chapter 6 (Bangkok, ILO/ROAP, unpublished).

Table 4.6: Percentage of male and female students enrolled in 1997*

Level	Percentage		Total
	Female	Male	
Kindergarten	49.10	50.90	2,107,381
Primary	48.46	51.54	5,399,857
Secondary	47.50	52.50	2,348,878
High School	54.82	45.18	797,938
Total	48.85	51.15	10,654,054

Source: Ministry of Education, Government of Thailand.

* Excluding the schools in Bangkok which have a different system of data collection.

It is also difficult to assess women's access to workplace-based training in Thailand because no useful data exist. However, circumstantial evidence suggests the presence of structural discrimination against women. It is said that employers are often reluctant to provide training, citing arguments such as the presumed likelihood that a woman will resign in order to get married and have children, and unreliability because of family care responsibilities. Further-more, women often lack access to property, credit, legal services and government training programmes, making access to employment and self-employment opportunities difficult.

In terms of vocational training for women, the DSD is the main agency involved. Of the total numbers of 98,039 and 221,753 workers who participated in vocational training in 1995 and 1998 respectively, 29.4 per cent and 36.2 per cent were female (see Table 4.7). One reason for the low participation rates is that many of the courses conducted are for traditionally male occupations. Those courses which are more gender neutral have a larger proportion of female enrolments. Many women enrol in short courses in traditional subjects such as cooking and sewing. Higher participation rates of women in longer-term training exist only in fields such as financial and business management.

Table 4.7: Outputs of Vocational Training – Department of Skills Development

Activity	1995			1998			1999		
	Male	Female	Total	Male	Female	Total	Male	Female	Total
Total	69,174	28,865	98,039	141,421	80,332	221,753	178,006	96,451	274,457
Pre-employment training	15,900	2,059	17,959	60,324	24,904	85,228	88,555	22,845	111,400
Rural training	13,249	9,475	22,724	–	–	–	–	–	–
Upgrading training	22,944	8,204	31,148	77,465	52,911	130,376	85,620	71,221	156,841
Non-technical training	14,832	8,139	22,971	–	–	–	–	–	–
Personal skill development	2,249	988	3,237	3,632	2,517	6,149	3,831	2,385	6,216

Source: Skill Development Statistics, Fiscal Years 1997/99 and N. Theeravit. op. cit.

(b) Displaced workers

The financial crisis, as was noted earlier, exposed a number of weaknesses in the human resources development policies in Thailand, as well as in many other countries in the region. The first is the lack of provision for displaced workers in general. Traditionally, the family has provided the basic unit of security. However, the transformation of these societies by the sheer speed of economic growth means that the family network and its resources can no longer sustain members during periods of long-term unemployment. This is particularly the case with the migrant workers who now form a substantial proportion of the labour force. Thus, the need to introduce forms of social protection and re-training programmes for displaced workers has been high on the agenda of the Thai Government.

The DSD has been entrusted with organizing retraining programmes for the unemployed and laid-off workers, with financial assistance from a number of international agencies. Under the World Bank social investment programme, there are plans to retrain 105,000 laid-off workers over the 1999 to 2000 period. The Asian Development Bank has developed a special programme to provide computer training for 10,000 laid-off workers through 16 universities nationwide. The Miyazawa Fund has been used to recruit 39 unemployed graduates as assistant coordinators in the organizing skill development programmes. The Government's own regular budget has been used for a similar exercise involving 295 unemployed graduates.

It is difficult to assess the impact of the various retaining and unemployment relief programmes as there have been no scientific evaluations of the outcomes of the training, and it is difficult to design and develop effective and efficient retraining programmes in such a short period of time. This often means that existing courses are modified for training laid-off workers without sufficient time to assess the needs of the labour market. Another limiting factor is that many laid-off workers are older workers with low education and skill levels. It is extremely difficult, if not impossible to retrain these workers for new jobs in the emerging high-technology industries.

(c) People with disabilities

At present, training for people with disabilities in Thailand is mainly provided in special centres catering solely for this target group. Currently, there are seven such centres run by the Department of Public Welfare in different parts of the country, with an eighth centre due to be opened in the coming months, and a further ten training centres operated by NGOs. The training capacity of these centres is limited, however, and some centres are operating significantly under capacity.

The quality of the training provided is constrained by the lack of a standard curriculum and by the relatively basic standard of the training in question, with the result that trainees may not be adequately prepared for work which they will be required to do in open employment.

The decisions on curriculum development do not seem to be based in any systematic way on links to the labour market locally or regionally. In recent years, a decision has been taken to promote access for disabled people to mainstream training centres as a way of expanding vocational training opportunities for disabled people, who are not catered for adequately at present.

There does not appear to be a nationally planned, adequately resourced approach, involving preparation of trainers as well as adaptation of the training premises and the training equipment and materials, if necessary. The Ministry of Education also provides education and training – in special schools – to people with certain disability types, including intellectual disability, visual and hearing impairment and physical disability. Some of these have initiated a policy of "reverse integration" recently, admitting non-disabled persons. This model, which combines vocational training in a range of activities including agricultural activities, animal husbandry, handicrafts and personal services with the educational curriculum from a certain age onwards, appears to have improved the success of the transition from school to working life for many school-leavers who started work on leaving or went on to further training. This approach merits further study as a model for the educational and training system as a whole, and as a way of improving the transition from school to working life for school leavers.

(d) Poverty alleviation in rural areas

The experience in many countries has shown that skill development can play a major role in the alleviation of poverty when it is carefully planned and implemented in the context of the available and emerging employment- and income-generation opportunities. Skill development, particularly for socially and economically disadvantaged target groups, has been found to be most successful when it has been used as a key component of an integrated employment generation and poverty alleviation strategy. The DSD has begun operating training in rural areas to assist people in finding non-agricultural jobs. This training is implemented on a mobile basis.

4.4 Policy Recommendations

Many of the issues raised in this chapter were discussed at the ILO Tripartite National Workshop on Training for Recovery: A Review of Training Policies, Programmes and Systems to Facilitate Economic Recovery.[15] The workshop also helped to identify policy priorities.

While the development of a new Vocational Education and Training Act will provide the legal basis for the reform of the TVE system, it is essential that a broad-ranging national vocational training strategy is developed, taking account of the ILO Human Resources Development Convention, 1975 (No. 142), and Recommendation 1975 (No. 150). The strategy should provide vision and direction for all the stakeholders involved in vocational training. It should provide guidance on areas of responsibility, delineate responsibility for provision of education and training to particular agencies based on their respective comparative advantages, and identify a framework for coordination. Furthermore, the national strategy should provide guidance on questions of access and equity, the role of the private sector and the financing of vocational training, as well as addressing the structural and legislative changes necessary to expand and improve the quality of skill training. Three specific recommendations are presented below for improving policy coordination, training policy initiatives and the role of the private sector. In order to promote economic competitiveness consistent with decent working conditions, the coordination mechanism of the present vocational training institutions should be improved. Furthermore, the present vocational training system should be extended to take into account the rapid increase in demand for skilled labour, the need for small and medium-sized enterprises and the promotion of gender equality. The role of the private sector should be assessed in the light of partnership with the public sector, or of public support for private sector training schemes.

---

[15] The workshop was held 17-18 March, 1999 at Amari Watergate Hotel, Bangkok.

4.4.1 Improving system-wide coordination

(a) A national policy development and coordination mechanism established either through reform and/or consolidation of existing NVTCC structure

As noted earlier, there is also an urgent need to improve the existing policy-making and coordination capacity of the vocational training system. This should be an ongoing process, not a one-off event. Ineffective coordination between training providers has been a problem for a long time. All options should be considered to develop the most appropriate mechanism for policy development and coordination of vocational training in Thailand.

(b) A national competency-based skill recognition, testing and certification system, structured around industrial training boards, with clearly identified industrial competencies

The lack of an effective national system of skill recognition is a major constraint to developing a skilled workforce. The present system of occupational skill standards is outdated and in urgent need of major reform. Many countries in the region have followed the global trend to competency-based systems of skill recognition linked to clearly identified industrial competencies. Australia and New Zealand already have established systems and Singapore is about to establish a new competency-based system. These systems have been in place in Europe for some time. The establishment of industrial training boards is a key element of these systems. Recognising the importance of the need for the national skill recognition system to adopt a competency-based approach, the DSD, through its Occupational Skill Standards Division is participating in the development of the ILO/Asian and Pacific Skill Development Programme's new Regional Model Competency Standards (RMCS). The DSD staff prepared and presented a pilot RMCS on the automotive service sector at a recent ILO/APSDEP regional meeting in the Republic of Korea.

4.4.2 Training policy initiatives

(a) Core work skills as a basis for further training

As a basis for training strategies, the Thai Government needs to secure what have been described as "core work skills" or broad competencies – the ability to communicate clearly in writing and to use mathematics and science skills to diagnose and solve problems – for the workforce. It is believed that these competencies have an important effect on immediate productivity, and also affect the ability of workers to learn new skills throughout their working lives. This adds the element of lifelong learning to the concept.[16]

(b) An expanded dual training programme

DOVE's Dual Vocational Training Project appears to be a promising source of skilled workers who will possess considerable industrial experience upon completion of their training. There are very few other long-term skilled worker training programmes which combine industrial and institutional training components. The programme will need to be expanded considerably if it is to have a significant impact at the national level. A substantial attitude change would also need to take place in many enterprises, so that more enterprises train, and train beyond their immediate needs.

---

[16] The Training for Recovery Workshop stressed this need.

(c) Improve and expand DSD's pre-employment training programme into a national apprentice training system

In a similar manner to the DOVE Dual Vocational Training Project, the pre-employment programmes of the DSD could be modified and expanded into a national apprentice system, with alternating periods of enterprise- and institution-based training. The existing courses already have an attachment to enterprises as a component.

(d) Greater access to training for small enterprises

Small enterprises often lack the resources or facilities to provide training. Furthermore, training institutions have not attempted to target small enterprises by providing them with the kind of training and flexibility needed. A major finding of the analysis of the operation of small and medium-sized companies is that the competitive capabilities of small firms are crucially affected by the quality of inter-firm and firm-institution networks in which the small firms are embedded.[17] Consequently, policy attention is now focused on establishing networks or sectoral clusters of firms, rather than on dealing with enterprises solely on an individual basis. Three specific types of inter-firm networks could be appropriate for Thailand: business networks, commodity chains, and sectoral clusters.

(e) A national adult education programme to develop the general education skills of Thai workers and, in particular, older workers

The relatively low level of general education of Thai workers, particularly older workers, is well known. The new Education Act will concentrate on expanding and improving the quality of the present education system. Those presently in the workforce will not benefit from this initiative and will require a different approach. A concerted national campaign to improve the general education and skills of workers who were not able to continue at school should be a high priority for both the Government and enterprises. There have been many successful examples of these types of programmes including Singapore's Basic Education for Skill Training and Worker Improvement through Secondary Education schemes. The Department of Non-Formal Education could play an important role in providing technical support to enterprises to develop adult education programmes in the workplace.

(f) Catering for the special needs of women workers

With a view to improving women's access to decent work in the formal and informal sectors, it is crucial to ensure that the major government programmes in the fields of TVE and VT become more gender responsive. Special attention needs to be given to increasing women's access to training in general and special measures are needed in fields where pronounced gender inequality is known to exist. Specific consideration needs to be given to:

(i) encouraging girls and young women to enrol in training in the science, technology, business and finance fields;

(ii) upgrading the training in traditionally female skills to lead to productive income-earning opportunities;

---

[17] F. Pyke. 1998. *Small firms, industrial relations and new roles for employers' and workers' organizations*, Background paper for 1997-98 World Labour Report (Geneva, ILO).

(iii) providing productive skills and entrepreneurial training in combination with credit and business support services to especially vulnerable groups of women – including retrenched women workers with little education, girls and young women prone to becoming involved in the sex trade or other types of labour exploitation and girls and women rescued from such abusive work;

(iv) providing accommodation facilities which encourage women's participation in training and a training environment which is free from sexual harassment.

4.4.3 The role of the private sector

(a) Establishing selected industry-based training centres

The development of industry-based training institutes for key selected industries could greatly facilitate Thai competitiveness. In addition to providing training and developing a competent workforce within the industry, these institutes could play a key role as industry research and development centres. The Penang Skill Development Centre in Malaysia is a well-known example in Asia.[18]

(b) A de-regulated system of training provision – public and private training providers competing for public and private training contracts

In many developed economies, governments are stepping back from the direct provision of training and, instead, playing a facilitating role and encouraging public training institutions to compete with private sector providers for training contracts. This approach has both positive and negative implications, but it is worth exploring as a possible long-term option.

(c) An expanded system of tax incentives and other financial measures to further promote training within enterprises

Under the Vocational Training Promotion Act, 1994, there is already tax relief for firms that provide training. But, as noted earlier, there is a relatively small number of firms participating. The related system to encourage firms in the private sector to register as private training providers is even more under-utilized, with less than 40 firms participating. It is not clear why more firms which are already providing training do not participate in these systems. These systems should be studied, evaluated and then modified to make them more effective and ensure the widest possible coverage. The DSD, however, as noted earlier, has recently announced that it is revising the Act to encourage more enterprises to join the scheme, provide more coverage and offer more benefits to the enterprises.

(d) An expanded system of accreditation and registration of private training providers

The Government has indicated its strong support for the expansion of private sector training. A major concern, however, is the quality and standard of many private training institutions. An expanded system of registering private training providers and accrediting their programmes is essential if the public is to be protected from ineffective and low-quality courses.

---

[18] The Penang Skill Development Centre for the electronics industry is based on a partnership between states, private enterprise and academia. The centre was established by multinational enterprises and the Penang State Government and is managed as a business by a management council composed of public and private sector representatives.

(e)   A series of pilot public and private partnerships and alliances in training

In order to promote greater training at the enterprise level, the government training agencies should actively offer their services to enterprises and assist in the development of workplace-based training programmes. There are already many interesting examples of this type of activity, including several completed by the DSD, but they are not widely known. These should be published as case-studies and promoted as examples of good practice worthy of replication.

Chapter 5
Social dialogue and employment issues

Social dialogue refers to any exchange of views among organized interest groups in the labour market on the social and labour market implications of economic trends and policies. This dialogue can take many forms, ranging from ad hoc and informal to more formal and permanent institutions for discussion or negotiation. Participants are similarly varied. In most countries of the world they include long-standing labour market actors – trade unions and employers' organizations. Social dialogue may also include any agency of representation, such as elected employee representatives, mass organizations, such as Thailand's Forum of the Poor, or other non-governmental organizations dealing with particular labour market concerns, e.g. child labour and women's access to jobs.

This section, however, will focus in particular on the most institutionalized forms of dialogue, which is to say those that are associated with a country's formal industrial relations system.

5.1 Social partners

Neither employers' organizations nor trade unions in Thailand are highly organized. Thailand has not ratified either the Freedom of Association and Protection of the Right to Organize Convention, 1948 (No. 87), or the Right to Organize and Collective Bargaining Convention, 1949 (No. 98). Stronger institutions and more effective legislation would enable Thai enterprises to better meet new challenges of international competition through social dialogue and collective bargaining.

5.1.1 Government agencies

The Ministry of Labour and Social Welfare was established in 1993. Its mission includes skill development, promoting employment and income and laying the foundations for social welfare and social security.[1] The activities of the Ministry are obviously no substitute for industrial relations and dispute resolution in the private sector.

Other government bodies dealing with labour relations include: the National Labour Advisory Development Council, which is a tripartite forum created to look into labour problems and present advice and proposals to the government; the National Wage Committee, which sets the minimum wage rates based on cost-of-living studies; and the Labour Relations Committee and a national system of labour courts, both of which are empowered to mediate on labour disputes. The Labour Relations Committee deals primarily with very serious disputes, which are considered threats to the national economy and national security. The labour courts mediate on individual grievances between employers and employees.[2]

---

[1] MOLSW, International Affairs Division, Profile Doc.

[2] ILO. 1997a. *Country Briefing Note: Thailand*, p. 17 (Bangkok, ILO-BAO, restricted).

5.1.2 Employers' organizations

Thailand's two major employers' organizations are the Employers' Confederation of Thailand (ECOT) and the Employers' Confederation of Thai Trade and Industry (ECONTHAI). It has been suggested that the representation of employers' interests in matters relating to labour and manpower could be considerably improved if both could merge. In any event, working together more closely would enhance their effectiveness.

Current laws contribute to significant fragmentation of employers' organizations. For example, a regulation that serves to weaken employers' organizations is the one that prohibits individual enterprises from becoming full members. They are limited to associate membership.

Serious fragmentation and limited membership mean that no single organization has the strength and resources to conduct serious research on policy issues. This weakness means that they are not always in a position to make a strong contribution to tripartite discussions. Quite often employers join an industrial organization and another group at the same time. The latter may be an organization such as a chamber of commerce that provides a network to suppliers and distributors.

Of course, organizations could also be strengthened by improving management, generating revenue, expanding roles, widening services and in this way attracting members.

5.1.3 Trade unions

There are three major national trade union centres in Thailand. These are the Labour Congress of Thailand (LCT), the Thai Trade Union Congress (TTUC) and the National Congress of Thai Labour (NCTL). While the LCT and the TTUC are affiliated with the International Confederation of Free Trade Unions (ICFTU) and its regional organization, the ICFTU-APRO (Asian and Pacific Regional Organization), the NCTL is affiliated with the World Council of Labour (WCL) and its regional structure, the Brotherhood of Asian Trade Unionists (BATU). The other important organization is the State Enterprise Workers' Relations Confederation (SERC), which is a grouping of trade unions in state-owned enterprises (SOEs). Trade unions in the SOEs were dissolved by the military government in 1991 and replaced by "associations". Under the labour legislation as it then stood, the SERC was not a registered body – the legislation did not allow for the registration of a federation of unions existing in SOEs. Associations formed in SOEs were restricted to enterprise-based status, and could extend membership coverage only to the workers employed in that enterprise.

The situation changed on 8 April 2000, when new legislation came into force. This was the end result of Parliament's 16 February 2000 move to pass the long-awaited State Enterprise Labour Relations Act, allowing the formation of trade unions in SOEs. The new Act has paved the way for a stronger trade union movement within Thailand, although it still does not provide the right to strike. It is estimated that more than 300,000 workers in SOEs will benefit from the new Act. There are currently 43 SOE trade unions – in a country with 61 SOEs.

Trade unions are also involved in campaigning for another piece of draft legislation – the Labour Relations Bill. This Bill is a revised draft of the Labour Relations Act, 1975. The Thai trade union movement has written to the ILO's Committee on Freedom of Association, pointing out the deficiencies of this Bill. Unions claim that this legislation is not based on international standards and denies basic union and worker rights.

The trade union movement in Thailand is comparatively weak in terms of its capacity to protect and promote the interests and rights of workers. The present unionization rate of around 3 per cent of the formal sector workforce is quite low. In addition, the multiplicity of trade union federations reflects the fragmented nature of the trade union movement. This fragmentation makes it very difficult for unions to mount any united front to deal with national issues such as the revision of labour legislation or opposition to policies on privatization of SOEs.

The economic crisis has also affected union membership, leading to an increasing number of workers losing their jobs. Moreover, economic restructuring and privatization policies have resulted in massive layoffs. Some prominent union officials have also lost their jobs. Under Thai labour legislation, once unemployed, they cannot continue to hold union positions. This has obviously affected the capacity of leadership. It has had a demoralizing effect on other union leaders as well.

5.2 Factors explaining weak labour organization

While weak trade unionism and relative under-representation of the labour force are common in Southeast Asia, Thailand has the lowest union density of all. Several factors may account for this. It is difficult to assess the independent significance of each, although the list would include the following:

Uneven policy support for freedom of association: Thailand shares with other countries in the East Asian region a history of political governance in which public policy support for freedom of association has not been consistent. Numerous military-dominated governments in the post Second World War era have often been accompanied by episodes of labour repression. The most recent of these, in 1991, resulted in a ban on trade unions in the state-owned sector, and thus an abrupt, 50 per cent decline in total union membership. The strength of the Thai labour movement lay traditionally in the public sector unions, and some have argued that the ban, which lasted until 2000, had a chilling effect on trade unionism as a whole.

State dominance in the labour market: The role played by the State in Thailand, as elsewhere in the region, involves a higher degree of public intervention in some areas of private labour market regulation than is usual in industrialized countries. This is particularly evident in the settlement of labour disputes, where both law and expectations combine to give the Ministry of Labour and Social Welfare a high profile. This reliance on the State rather than private mechanisms for dispute resolution – such as negotiation, well-developed grievance procedures at enterprise level and industrial action – may have played a part in preventing Thai trade unions from assuming the same role as their counterparts in other parts of the world.

Loopholes in the legal and administrative framework: In general, the Labour Relations Act, 1975 places no major constraints on (private-sector) trade union formation. The threshold number of employees required to form a trade union (ten persons) is not an obstacle. The law also offers clear legal protection to trade unions once they have been established. However, the protection offered to trade union organizers is less significant. The law does not act as a major deterrent to employers who want to frustrate trade union organization. As one trade union official observed: "It is easier in Thailand to form a labour federation than a trade union".[3] Second, although the law does not place unreasonable constraints on the scope of bargaining subjects, it does give the State considerable discretion to curb collective negotiations.

---

[3] Statement made at the ILO National Tripartite Forum on Thailand at a Crossroads, November 1997.

The freedom to strike, for example, is proscribed in a generous number of industries deemed either essential, or vital to national security. Collective negotiations can also be suspended on the grounds of unfavourable economic conditions.

The proliferation of labour federations, and the competition and fragmentation that this has produced may have something to do with the ease with which they can be formed – but it has, perhaps, more to do with the incentive to do so. Labour representation on Thailand's tripartite bodies is decided using a one union/one vote rule – and it is this which provides the incentive. It rewards federations comprising many small trade unions, irrespective of the number of actual employees they represent. As long as competition for a limited number of seats in the broader political arena is seen to offer greater rewards than offering good, direct service to rank-and-file trade union members through collective bargaining, the leadership of the Thai labour movement risks remaining divided – less by ideology than by personal ambition – and distracted from the task of direct representation of their members' interests.

Economic factors working against labour organization: The growth of the industrial workforce is still relatively recent. It resulted in the migration of the rural population to urban industrial locations, where there was no tradition of labour organization in a factory setting. The insecurity of migrant workers may make them reticent to exercise their legal rights. Evidence suggests that ignorance of those legal rights is also common. Just as the existence of a labour surplus erodes the collective strength of labour, particularly unskilled labour, so does the opposite – a tight labour market when jobs and earnings have been increasing at impressive annual rates. This may have diminished the perceived need for trade union representation and collective bargaining, since growth alone provided satisfactory outcomes. Workers who were dissatisfied were able to find new jobs offering acceptable and often increasing wages, and it seems reasonable to assume that this made turnover an acceptable alternative to voice mechanisms. It is also possible that trade union organization faces less resistance when industrialization occurs through a more sheltered process of import-substitution than when it is export-oriented. In the latter instance, labour costs may be more likely to be disciplined by the forces of international markets. Export orientation may be a factor, therefore, in increasing employer opposition to trade union organization.

Cultural and religious factors: Observers of Thai industrial relations often invoke cultural and religious factors to explain the weakness of trade unions and collective bargaining. According to them, the central part that Buddhism plays in Thai culture, its advocacy of the middle path or avoidance both of extremes and of direct confrontation, are inconsistent with trade union organization and rational or direct decision-making through collective bargaining. The same religious norms are also thought to favour third-party (i.e. State) intervention in instances in which disputes do arise that would otherwise lead to direct confrontation. Similarly, these norms may imply a preference for more cooperative or consensual mechanisms for labour-management dialogue than for collective bargaining. Social relations in Thailand, including those at the workplace, are frequently said to follow a patron-client pattern. Employees' hierarchical obedience and loyalty are in turn rewarded by the employers' loyalty and responsibility.

5.3 The extent of dialogue: A statistical overview

In at least some important ways an already weak industrial relations system has become still weaker as a result of the economic downturn. This discussion turns first, however, to the general level, describes the channels through which labour market adjustment occurs, and then to the effects of the Asian financial crisis on industrial relations institutions in Thailand.

As noted, the banning of trade unions and collective bargaining in SOEs at the beginning of the decade halved union membership in Thailand.[4] Since then, however, in a climate of political liberalization and economic growth, both the number of trade unions and union membership has been rising progressively, albeit from low initial levels. Table 5.1 shows trends in the number of registered trade unions in the 1990s. Trends in actual trade union membership are given.

The regional distribution of trade unions gives the appearance of a trend toward greater geographical dispersion. In fact, however, when the five industrial provinces` surrounding Bangkok are taken together with Bangkok, it is clear that trade unionism continues to be highly concentrated in the greater metropolitan area of Bangkok.

Table 5.1: Numbers of trade unions, collective bargaining agreements and employees' committees in Thailand

Year	Public-sector unions	Total number of unions	Union members	New unions	Disbanded unions
1972	2	9	n.a.	9	0
1973	4	22	n.a.	13	0
1974	11	45	n.a.	23	0
1975	28	111	50,000	66	0
1976	49	184	70,483	78	5
1977	47	164	n.a.	2	22
1978	54	174	95,951	23	13
1979	62	206	114,349	52	20
1980	70	255	150,193	55	6
1981	79	334	153,960	90	11
1982	84	376	214,636	58	15
1983	91	414	221,739	47	10
1984	93	430	212,343	45	29
1985	97	436	214,359	56	50
1986	107	469	241,709	59	26
1987	116	514	272,608	69	24
1988	118	562	295,901	77	29
1989	123	593	309,041	71	40
1990	130	713	336,061	142	22
1991	0	657	169,424	102	158
1992	0	749	190,142	136	44
1993	0	839	231,480	130	40
1994	0	888	242,730	129	80
1995	0	971	261,348	104	21
1996	0	1,015	280,963	86	45
1997	0	968	270,276	57	104
1998	0	999	265,982	71	40

Source: MOLSW. *Yearbook of Labour Statistics*, various years, and unpublished data.

---

[4] It did not, however, silence workers' voices, as 1999's protests over privatization have shown. Social dialogue and the public sector will be discussed below.

In 1997, the number of trade unions declined for the first time this decade, a movement likely to be a reflection of the initial effects of the crisis following its onset in July 1997. The decline was particularly concentrated: the greatest share of the decline occurred in only one province, the industrial province of Pathum Thani, where the number of registered unions decreased from 148 to 87 over the 12-month period to December 1997.

By law, trade union organization in Thailand is by enterprise or by industry. Very gradually in the 1990s, the share of industry unions in the total had been increasing. It moved from 43 to 44 per cent in the first half of the decade, to 46 per cent in 1996, and 48 per cent in 1997. It is probable that the crisis and associated business closures have affected the most recent shift in relative shares of trade union types. The number of enterprise unions declined by 9 per cent in 1997 over the previous year, whereas the number of industry unions held almost constant. Economic conditions have different effects on different trade union structures, and enterprise unions are more vulnerable to severe downturns than other trade union structures.

The Labour Relations Act, 1975 allows for (but does not mandate) the creation of employee committees in establishments with more than 50 employees. Collective bargaining and employee committees constitute the two main formal[5] channels for collective labour-management dialogue at enterprise level. (The Labour Protection Act, 1998 also mandates the establishment of employee welfare committees.) As with trade unions, the number of employee committees grew over the 1990s, and their decline in 1997 may also reflect the impact of the crisis. There are 24,830 establishments employing more than 50 persons in Thailand. Employee committees thus exist in only 2 per cent of their potential locations. There are 610 establishments employing more than 1,000 persons in Thailand. Assuming, in the absence of information, that the employee committees are all located in these large firms and assuming further that the average establishment size in this category is, say, 1,200 employees, then employee committees would still only affect about 8 per cent of Thailand's formal private-sector workforce. This estimate is an extreme upper bound, however, and the assumptions on which it is based are unlikely to be true. The real number of employees covered by this particular voice mechanism is thus almost certain to be lower, perhaps much lower. Moreover, the vast majority of employee committees exist in establishments that also have trade unions.[6] The two means of participation are therefore not substitutes. If they were, a larger share of the workforce would be covered by at least one voice mechanism.

However small, relative to the size of the Thai workforce, the number of trade unions nevertheless greatly exceeds the number of collective bargaining agreements (see Table 5.2). Since collective bargaining exists at the enterprise level in Thailand, between a single employer and a single enterprise or industrial union, it can be concluded that the majority of Thai trade unions have no collective bargaining agreement with their employer. This means that, while trade union membership is already a small share of the total workforce, collective bargaining coverage is even smaller – and since the crisis, smaller still. The number of collective agreements fell sharply in the recession year of 1997, from 381 in 1996 to 271 by December 1997. The data on submission of trade union demands also include the number of workers affected by the demands. Over the past three years, an average of 450 workers have been affected by each demand for collective negotiation. Using that number as a "guesstimate" of

---

[5] Formal in the sense of provided for and regulated by law, unlike, for example, quality circles.

[6] Sungsidh Piriyarangsan. 1998. *Bipartite Systems: Workplace relations in Thailand*, Report prepared for ILO/ EASMAT (Bangkok).

Table 5.2: Numbers of employee committees and registered collective agreements in Thailand

Year	Number of employee committees	Number of registered collective agreements
1991	394	275
1992	442	233
1993	526	275
1994	453	337
1995	477	375
1996	523	381
1997	510	271

Source: MOLSW. *Yearbook of Labour Statistics*, various years, and unpublished data.

the number of workers actually covered by a collective agreement, the result is just under 122,000 for December 1997 – or about 1.6 per cent of the formal private sector workforce.

The evidence suggests that the formal institutional participation of Thai workers in decisions made by employers affecting their jobs and remuneration during the crisis was minimal, if not negligible. Of course, such dialogue as might have occurred to mitigate the social costs of the crisis cannot be fully described by the observations above. These refer, after all, only to the enterprise level.

Social dialogue on employment options during the crisis also occurred at the national tripartite level. Also, the data above refer only to what can be quantified – the number of unions or collective agreements, for example – and say little of the true climate for social dialogue in Thailand, for example, any changes in the actual quality of the labour-management relationship. Finally, it would be wrong to think that social dialogue can only occur through formal mechanisms. Informal norms and behaviours cannot be ignored. If fewer jobs were lost in the crisis than anticipated, it may be that culture, norms of behaviour, implicit contracts and informal channels of communication played a role in labour market adjustment in this period.

5.4 Tripartism in Thailand and the crisis

Thailand has 16 national tripartite consultative or decision-making bodies, whether established by law or by Cabinet resolution. These cover a broad range of mandates in labour market management, from workplace safety to minimum wage determination to dispute settlement. The fact that tripartite machinery exists is not a measure of its effectiveness, and in Thailand as elsewhere there is clear scope for improvement if tripartism is to play a strengthened role in the dialogue on economic and social policy choices.

Chief among the weaknesses of tripartism in Thailand is the obvious point that tripartism can only be as strong as its constituent parts. Fragmented interest groups with low membership levels risk losing credibility, and may not be able to act as an effective voice for the workforce's concerns. In practice, this is reflected in Thailand by the dominant position that Government frequently assumes in tripartite consultations. Weak constituent parts weaken the effective uses to which tripartism can be put. The Thai trade unions' own evaluation of the present weaknesses of tripartism is shown in Box 5.1.

The general pattern of how Thailand's labour market has adjusted to the crisis has been discussed earlier in this report. In technical terms, the Thai labour market experienced a substantial amount of downward wage flexibility and numerical flexibility. Downward wage flexibility in the form of wage and salary reductions was common. Numerical flexibility – defined as adjustment in the *quantity* of labour input – generally occurred in two ways: adjustments either in the number of persons working, or in the hours that they worked.[7] The perhaps surprising outcome of the crisis in Thailand is that job loss was not as pronounced as originally foreseen. Rather, enterprises appear to have engaged in labour hoarding, retaining workers but cutting the hours of work.

The crisis has weakened some of the building blocks on which social dialogue is founded, among them union membership. At the same time, however, the crisis has also served to reinvigorate or add momentum to some joint approaches to problem solving. Two tripartite mechanisms are worthy of particular discussion – the National Wage Committee and the National Labour Development Advisory Council (NLDAC) – since these have the closest bearing on employment policy. The Government also took measures in response to the crisis when the Prime Minister moved in December 1997 to form a Committee on the Alleviation of Unemployment. However, the process cannot be described as a truly robust example of tripartite social dialogue. Worker and employer representation on the Committee was minimal, and it is unclear what contribution their presence made to the final shape of the initiatives proposed. The initiatives were placed under the responsibility of individual ministries. Programme implementation did not specify a role for the social actors, nor has the process of implementation apparently been a tripartite one.

---

[7] This issue is discussed in detail in Sununta Siengthai. 1999. *Industrial Relations and the recession in Thailand*, Report prepared for the Thailand CEPR (Bangkok, ILO/EASMAT).

5.4.1 The National Wage Committee and the minimum wage

An important instance of the influence of social dialogue on employment policy in Thailand is through the mechanism of how wages are determined. At the micro level, wage fixing in Thai enterprises might be considered to be set by market forces, mediated through individual bargaining power and unilateral employer determination. The limited extent of collective bargaining, as earlier noted, would seem to add weight to such a view. It is, however, quite misleading, as wage setting in Thailand has been powerfully guided by frequent adjustments to a nationally determined, three-tier minimum wage. These adjustments are the result of the deliberations of the tripartite National Wage Committee on which equal numbers of workers', employers', and government representatives sit, and whose recommendations are commonly accepted by the Government.

It is through the Committee that social dialogue in Thailand has its most significant effect on macroeconomic policy choices. Whereas the crisis in Malaysia and in the Republic of Korea has to varying degrees led to national social dialogue over a broad range of macro-economic policies, including fiscal and monetary policies; social dialogue in Thailand is confined to minimum wage adjustments. As a tool of employment policy, moreover, the National Wage Committee cannot be considered a full-blown incomes policy mechanism. Although the law requires that minimum wage adjustments must take into account inflationary effects and anticipate employment impacts, among other factors, it does not empower the Committee to set inflation targets or employment objectives.

Minimum wage trends and the problem of low labour productivity growth were discussed in Chapter 1. With respect to the wage-setting *process*, two points are worthy of mention. First, one effect of the minimum wage policy in Thailand is that the minimum wage appears to apply to far more persons than just unskilled, new entrants to the workforce. Trade union officials complain that workers with long records of service and improved skills are "stuck" at the minimum wage level. Employers complain that they are unable to reward employees through an internal, enterprise wage policy, because minimum wage adjustments reduce their capacity to offer enterprise-based wage increases. The evidence supports both: there is a quite substantial share of workers earning the minimum wage who have three or four years of experience on the job. It is possible that, while the minimum wage policy in Thailand has brought clear benefits, it may also have unintentionally played a part in displacing enterprise-based mechanisms for wage determination. It is plausible, for example, that workers have relied on national wage decisions rather than seeking enterprise-based social dialogue through trade unions and collective bargaining. This could be a factor undermining efforts at labour organization, since some of the incentive for trade union membership is diminished. On the employers' side, it is possible that minimum wage adjustments have discouraged them from developing more comprehensive, enterprise-based wage policies. Minimum wage policy might also work against the development of wage and personnel policies seeking to reward perform-ance, build commitment, improve productivity, etc. These are issues that future wage policy needs to explore further and address.

The second procedural issue involving minimum wage fixing concerns the 1998 decision to decentralize minimum wage fixing to the provincial level. Under the terms of the yet-to-be implemented decision, the National Wage Committee retains its responsibility for setting a national basic minimum wage as the lowest threshold or wage floor, but provinces themselves recommend, on the basis of several specific, statutory criteria, a proportional increase to be applied as the provincial minimum wage. The Committee can accept, amend, or reject the provincial recommendation.

Thai trade unions have expressed concern over decentralization of wage fixing. Newly established provincial wage committees would be, like the National Wage Committee, tripartite in structure. The concern, however, is that trade union organization is particularly thin outside the Bangkok metropolitan area and the neighbouring five provinces. Therefore, it would be difficult to ensure legitimate and competent worker participation in provincial social dialogue on wages. As a result, the minimum wage could be eroded or its growth slowed.[8] There is still no experience with the new system. The ILO has taken an active role in meeting the requisite training needs for some of the new provincial committee members, including training on how to conduct tripartite negotiations and training on the criteria for wage determination and adjustment. It is too early, of course, to claim that trade union concerns will prove unjustified. It is even possible that the provincial wage committees will help extend and strengthen tripartism in Thailand.

5.4.2 The National Labour Advisory Development Council

Like the National Wage Committee, the NLADC is one of a minority of tripartite bodies enjoying equal representation from among the tripartite constituents. It is the country's main tripartite body and has the broadest mandate of all in the area of labour policy. Although it is a consultative body, it can influence Government actions.[9] Throughout the months of the economic downturn, deliberations within the NLADC have produced a variety of recommendations to the Government on economic and social policy measures. The Council undertook an investigation of the consequences of the crisis on job loss, incomes, the educational system, health, safety and political stability. On the basis of its review of the impact, the NLADC made recommendations in three main areas, including job creation and social development, enhancing development potential for rural communities and extending the State's welfare system.

One recommendation was that the State agencies delivering public services, such as education, health, etc., should extend the reach of their services by using volunteers from among the urban unemployed – people who did not want to return to their rural communities while they still had savings. Another recommendation focused on the commercial development of rural, agricultural communities. The NLADC proposed that the Government should provide technical assistance in marketing rural products, and encourage communities to use barter transaction systems rather than cash. The NLADC also recommended extending the Social Security Act, 1990's Article 38 to support access to health care and state subsidies for educational tuition and fees for the children of families affected by the recession. While there do not appear to be any impact analyses of the effects of various measures taken, some of the recommendations proposed by the NLADC do appear to have been implemented by the Government. The deliberations and recommendations of the NLADC extend beyond labour market concerns of the formal sector to income and livelihood issues in the informal sector.

---

[8] Employers, on the other hand, have sometimes expressed concern that, in the absence of an effective worker voice on the provincial committees, the Government partner might be compelled to adopt a worker viewpoint on wage-setting to the detriment of employers' labour cost considerations.

[9] The influence of the NLADC was affirmed in an interview with its Chairman, Khun Sawai Pramanee, November 1997.

5.5 Bipartism and the crisis

There is evidence that the crisis has altered at least some of the underlying conditions that had previously constrained the development of sound industrial relations at the enterprise level. First, both workers' and employers' organizations have explicitly endorsed the need to improve the exercise of freedom of association and promote bipartite relations.[10] Second, efforts to overcome the fragmentation of Thailand's trade union federations appear to have gathered momentum. In preparation for a tripartite national meeting on the financial crisis in November 1997,[11] for example, all eight of the major federations met over two days to adopt a coordinated strategy. Such instances of cooperation have been repeated since then. Third, commitment to dialogue that was emerging just before the crisis seems to have become stronger. Thailand's workers' and employers' organizations committed themselves to two codes of conduct. The 1996 Code of Conduct on Labour Relations committed Thailand's workers' and employers' organizations to finding ways to reduce industrial conflict and setting up mechanisms for bipartite dialogue. The 1998 Code of Practice to Promote Labour Relations strengthened this process, outlining ways in which workplace costs might be reduced, and committing parties to the principle that bipartite social dialogue was a necessary prerequisite to any decision affecting employees' welfare at the workplace.

Other evidence supports this trend. In 1998, a tripartite committee on workplace cooperation that had been formed under the Ministry of Labour and Social Welfare's auspices in the mid-1990s endorsed a variety of recommendations proceeding from a study of best-case examples by one of Thailand's leading industrial relations scholars.[12] Thailand's two main pieces of industrial relations legislation, directed respectively to the private and public sectors, are well advanced in the process of legislative reform. Each would improve the rights supporting bipartite social dialogue and expand the related institutions.

The climate for industrial democracy is strongly shaped by attitudes toward democratic governance in society at large. There can be little doubt that the process of constitutional reform in Thailand has enjoyed wide popular support and participation, and that the new Constitution of 1997 itself is unambiguous in its support for freedom of association and democratic governance. If anything, the crisis has reinforced these values, especially in the light of the general agreement that limitations on democratic governance played at least some part in the onset of the crisis.

There is also less pressure to improve bipartite relations when "the going is good" and the distribution of jobs and incomes is providing satisfactory outcomes. Improvements become more essential when conditions worsen and the need arises to generate understanding or face workplace unrest. The Confederation of Thai Trade and Industry (ECONTHAI) officials, for example, agreed that one effect of the crisis had been to improve the flow of information and

---

[10] Most recently, this occurred in the National Tripartite Workshop held (17 August 1999, Bangkok) to discuss this chapter's findings.

[11] ILO National Tripartite Forum on Thailand at a Crossroads, November 1997.

[12] Piriyarangsan Sungsidh. 1998. *Bipartite Systems: Workplace relations in Thailand*, Report prepared for ILO/EASMAT (Bangkok).

communication at the workplace.[13]   Additional support for this comes from enterprise case studies commissioned for this report, as discussed later.

Furthermore, as industries upgrade and their products, services and processes become more sophisticated, there is an associated tendency to move away from purely cost-based competitive advantage to exploiting a variety of non-price competitive assets, such as speed, quality, etc. This relies on the knowledge, skills and motivation of the workforce. Harnessing these requires a high level of openness, trust and communication and this in turn depends on the quality of bipartite social dialogue. Changes in product markets and technologies also create a need for enterprise-level dialogue and the information and communication flows that this dialogue allows.

For all these reasons, both the demand and the need for bipartite social dialogue appear likely to increase in Thailand. In preparing the present report, evidence was sought of changes in labour-management relations produced by the crisis. It cannot be claimed that the findings are representative in any statistical sense, but they do shed some light on adjustment options and the nature of bipartite social dialogue in the crisis. Highlights are shown in Table 5.3.

Conclusions cannot be drawn from just a few examples, but elements of the pattern of adjustment presented in this table are quite consistent with other statistical evidence on how Thailand has adjusted to the crisis.   In particular, shedding jobs does not emerge as the adjustment mechanism of choice. Of course, jobs have been lost. For example, an estimated 30 per cent of jobs in the auto industry (from manufacturing to dealer distribution) have been lost.   But, even here, this is against a reduction in business activity which, in the depths of the downturn, had fallen to approximately 28 per cent of its pre-crisis level.[14]

The enterprise-level study found that joint labour-management consultative mechanisms appear to have become valuable tools in crisis management, as it is primarily through these that the recorded increase in information exchange has occurred.   It is interesting to speculate whether consultative options might be preferred in the Thai context as, unlike the forms that collective bargaining can sometimes take, consultative mechanisms are less likely to involve direct confrontation.   A related observation from the study is that collective negotiations appeared to go more smoothly and rapidly when issues on the bargaining table had been subject to prior discussion in a joint consultative mechanism.   The banking and auto industry examples showed a relationship between the quality of the trade union-management relationship and the strength of the trade union (as reflected in the degree of support it enjoyed among the workforce).   In this context, quality means the credibility that the union has with management, and management's willingness to include the trade union as a true partner in problem-solving and decision-making.   There are clearly many elements that make for a good labour-management relationship, but a strong union was found to be one ingredient.

In view of the variety of forms that social dialogue can take, specific attention needs to be given to the role of trade unions. In the few examples offered above, it is clear that trade unions and labour-management consultation mechanisms were complements – consultation options were not used as substitutes for trade unions. The question remains, though, how to

---

[13] Comments made at a tripartite consultation on wage policy organized by the ILO/EASMAT in Bangkok, October 1998.

[14] Sununta Siengthai. op. cit., p. 49.

84

Table 5.3: Social dialogue, the enterprise and adjusting to the economic downturn: Some examples

	Background:	Crisis effect on labour-management dialogue:	Adjustment measures agreed through dialogue:
Example 1, an enterprise in the banking sector	Unionized. 26,000 employees. 60 per cent union members. Affected by crisis, but less severely than other major banks.	Marked increase in communication and information exchange through joint consultations. High degree of cooperation reported (first institutionalized by an abrupt 1984 business down-turn in the bank).	No involuntary layoffs. Bank-wide restructuring and negotiated internal redeploy-men. Reduction-of bonus from 5-6 months to 3 months. Early Retirement package for employees: 45 years old with 15 years' tenure for employees; 50 years old with 20 years' tenure for supervisors. Reduction in salary increase from 8-10 per cent to 3 per cent. Union withholds new demands for the present time. Increased skills training for employees and labour law training paid for by bank for union officials.
Example 2, an enterprise in the automotive sector	Unionized. 4,000 employees. 70 per cent union members. Sharp decline in business during the crisis	Marked increase in communication and information exchange through joint consultative committees.	Negotiations ongoing over wages and reduction in bonus. 1996 declaration on no strikes in return for greater company support to union. No involuntary layoffs. Increased job rotation. Increased company-funded training in parent company.
Example 3, an enterprise in the automotive sector	Unionized. 380 employees. 65 per cent union members. Sharp decline in business. (No new work from May 1997 till May 1999).	Marked increase in communication and information exchange through joint consultative committees.	No involuntary layoffs thus far 3 months' leave with statutory pay reduction (November 1998 – January 1999). Hiring freeze. Elimination of bonus. 10 per cent wage reduction for those earning over 5,000 baht per month.
Example 4, an example in the garment sector	Unionized. 1,200 employees. Export-oriented. The crisis had no effect on business.	Collective bargaining is annual and, in view of the stability of the business throughout the crisis, there has been no reported change in the frequency of labour-management dialogue.	**Adjustment measures agreed through dialogue:** No layoffs, and no additional measures.
Example 5, an example in the garment sector	Non-union. 700 employees. Export-oriented. The crisis had only a slight impact on business.	No effect reported. Company practices high degree of communication through informal channels, e.g. frequent management meetings with various groups of employees, and frequent meetings between supervisors and subordinates.	**Adjustment measures:** Current hiring freeze. No involuntary layoffs. Staff reduction through attrition. Units asked to reduce production costs. Efforts increased to find new product markets.

Source: Sumunta Siengtbai. op. cit.

85

ensure that such complementarity is the norm and not the exception. Of course, trade unions themselves have a responsibility here. They need to ensure among other things the continued relevance of the services they offer, and the quality and competence of their leadership. Many of these challenges are difficult as long as the unions remain relatively weak. For example, an estimated 90 per cent of Thai trade unions face financial difficulties which, in turn, make it difficult for them to perform the functions for which they were formed. Trade union effectiveness also depends on the extent to which their institutional security is protected and promoted by labour law. This point is made clear in the policy discussion below.

5.6 Policy recommendations

The two major recommendations are to strengthen tripartite machinery and develop bipartite relations. These require a number of steps, spelled out below. Points raised in this chapter were discussed in a national tripartite workshop in Bangkok on 17 August 1999. The policy recommendations are based on the needs identified at this workshop.

5.6.1 Strengthen tripartite machinery

It is generally acknowledged that tripartism in Thailand is weak. Some of this is due to the weakness of the tripartite constituents themselves. As to the weakness of tripartite machinery per se, the following factors appear the most important to address:

Ensure equal or at least much more balanced participation: The most successful tripartite mechanisms in Thailand, for example the Social Security Tripartite Committee, have a common feature – equal representation of the three constituents. When it is not equal, which is the case for several of the country's 16 mechanisms, the Government voice dominates at the expense of workers' and employers' contributions. Participants at the August workshop gave broad endorsement to the need for more balanced tripartite bodies. However, there were some differences over how this might be achieved. Worker participants argued that the practice of the same Government representatives sitting in different tripartite bodies should cease. The Ministry of Labour and Social Welfare disagreed, arguing, first, a shortage of qualified personnel for all bodies and, second, the advantage of a consistent the Government voice when fewer people are involved in many bodies.

Clarify and reinforce the authority of tripartite decisions: Another shared feature linking the most successful tripartite mechanisms in Thailand is the authoritative weight carried by their decisions. Tripartite decisions that are either ignored and not implemented, or unilaterally changed by the Government, run the risk of eroding the interest in and credibility of tripartism. The implication here is not that the full authority for decision-making be handed over to tripartite machinery. At a minimum, however, the mandate of each tripartite mechanism needs to be made very clear, and assurances are needed that decisions of tripartite bodies will not simply be ignored; and a reporting framework is needed that would oblige the Government to justify clearly the grounds for not implementing decisions reached through tripartite consultation.

Establish transparent, logical, and fair criteria for appointment to tripartite bodies and expand the scope of dialogue: It was widely agreed at the 1999 workshop that the selection of participants in tripartite bodies could be improved. The one union/one vote criterion for worker representation was identified as an issue – leading in practice to the absence of the labour federations which represented through their unions the largest number of union members.

Another factor was competence. Participants often lacked knowledge of the subject area for tripartite discussion. For both workers and employers, appointment to tripartite bodies needs to be made on the basis of explicit criteria of competence. As a supporting measure, the Government should consider establishing a formal training policy for participants in tripartite bodies. Training could address not only the substance of the issues dealt with by the tripartite mechanism, for example wage fixing, but also the tripartite decision-making processes themselves. Another effective method to strengthen the tripartite mechanism is to expand dialogue beyond tripartite representatives. Some worker participants at the August workshop felt that tripartism could be strengthened if representatives were able to bring in experts to help with their deliberations. The use of experts in tripartite machinery should be encouraged.

Review the scope of tripartite bodies: The range of subjects currently discussed in tripartite bodies could be reviewed. An employer participant observed that there was currently no tripartite mechanism in which employment policy was discussed. Establishing a body to fill this gap would allow for needed discussions of productivity improvement and training needs. The extent of tripartite discussion on minimum wage fixing could also be reviewed.

5.6.2. Develop bipartite relations

Tripartism can only be as effective as its individual constituents. Consequently, the growth of workers' and employers' organizations needs to be encouraged, first of all, and so do bipartite relations between the two. Parts of the agenda for reform rely on legislative change, as noted below.

Remove legal impediments to freedom of association: The country's main labour relations laws are currently under review. It is important that both the Labour Relations Act, 1975 and the State Enterprise Labour Relations Act, 2000 reflect strongly the guarantees of freedom of association embodied in Thailand's Constitution. In particular, loopholes permitting the victimization of labour organizers in the private sector should be closed.

An appropriate place to begin is through ratification of all ILO Conventions relating to industrial relations, including the Freedom of Association and Protection of the Right to Organize Convention, 1948 (No. 87), the Right to Organize and Collective Bargaining Convention, 1949 (No. 98), the Workers' Representatives Convention, 1971 (No. 135), the Rural Workers' Organizations Convention, 1975 (No. 141), the Labour Relations (Public Service) Convention, 1978 (No. 151), and the Collective Bargaining Convention, 1981 (No. 154). All six are consistent with the principles articulated in Thailand's new Constitution. Trade unions argue further that there should be one basic labour law applying to both the private and the state-owned sectors, rather than two laws as at present.

Reform procedures on the rights to association of workers and employers: An aspect of freedom of association refers to the formation of labour federations and employer organizations. In Thailand the excessive fragmentation of the labour movement is a problem, which, in turn, renders it difficult for labour to speak with a unified voice. The Government needs to rethink the legal framework governing the formation of labour federations with a view to encouraging the formation of larger, more comprehensive federations. At the same time, the Government needs to remove the incentive to fragmentation that currently exists in the form of the one union/one-vote system of appointing labour representatives to tripartite bodies. The country's labour laws should also place no prohibitions on trade unions in the public and private sectors becoming affiliates of the same labour federation. As for employers' organizations, these could be strengthened and their membership increased if the laws were changed to allow individual enterprises to become members of the peak employers' organizations. Another source of fragmentation among employers' organizations could be removed if these organizations were required to register under just one ministry, rather than, as at present, different ministries depending upon the function and or composition of the organization.

Extend the legal right to join a trade union to the unemployed: Thai legislation currently restricts trade union membership to those who are employed. In consequence, the loss of a job also means the loss of trade union membership. This restriction needs to be lifted. Doing so will give the unemployed an organized voice through which their interests can be represented. Another advantage is organizational continuity, particularly when the laid-off worker has been a union official.

Promote labour-management dialogue at enterprise level: The draft of the reformed Labour Relations Act on which the Ministry of Labour and Social Welfare is currently working would mandate the creation of labour-management councils in enterprises employing more than 15 persons. This is a positive step. The law needs to ensure that the election criteria and procedures for employee representatives are transparent and protected. It also needs to ensure that the employee representatives are protected in their function as councillors and guaranteed freedom of speech and action. Finally, the law needs to ensure that the role of trade unions at enterprise level is clearly included and protected in the functioning of the labour-management councils. In particular, the law needs to ensure that the councils do not displace collective bargaining and trade unions. During the August workshop, employers argued that there are now too many enterprise committees with different mandates. To economize on administrative time, they said, these should be rationalized into one committee.

Liberalize the use of collective bargaining and the right to strike: The current labour relations law places excessive constraints on the right to strike when bargaining comes to an impasse. The list of essential services and other industries in which the legal strike is curtailed needs to be revised and shortened. Similarly, current provisions that allow the state of the economy to be used as grounds for limiting the right to bargain collectively and to strike need to be removed or restricted. These changes would help reduce the role of the State in private-sector labour relations, encouraging more mature and healthier bipartite relations at enterprise level.

Improve knowledge of the role of trade unions and industrial relations: Many of the participants at the August workshop felt that employees and employers had little knowledge of the role of trade unions and collective bargaining and that trade unions had an "image problem". Obviously, there is a need – irrespective of policy reform – for the trade unions themselves to advance their own cause in a more effective way. Trade unions could be strengthened (and thus better able to service their members and organize new ones) if they were financially sound. Thought should be given to criteria for a "dues checkoff" system at the workplace. One employer participant said reform of the basic education system in Thailand was the best place to start, since Thai students were largely unaware of labour market institutions, and were not taught to think critically or to challenge received ideas – skills that underlie the concept of negotiation and compromise. Awareness of the role of trade unions and the importance of industrial relations could be improved if the government were to launch a media campaign focusing on unions and their role, as well as collective bargaining, pointing out that this is not only a public good but also a right enshrined in the Thai Constitution.

Chapter 6

Labour market information and active labour market policies

Implementation of the CEPR in Thailand comes during an economic crisis that has prompted a serious examination of policies and institutions. As part of their own review of the current economic situation and efforts to improve labour market policies, government agencies together with the social partners have demonstrated considerable interest in improving labour market information for purposes of policy analysis and social dialogue.

Several weaknesses in the labour market information (LMI) system were evident at the outset of the crisis: fragmentation of existing information; delayed processing and dissemination of this information; inadequate capacity on the part of concerned government agencies and social partners to analyse, interpret and use such information; and insufficient regular, reliable, transparent and timely information to identify issues, formulate policy, monitor projects and evaluate programmes.

Recent efforts to analyse the causes of economic conditions and suggest solutions for labour market problems have alerted users to these shortcomings in the information being produced and disseminated by various agencies. Better labour market information is required to identify trends in economic conditions and the labour market. This information is also essential for assessing existing and planned programmes for promoting job creation, enterprise development, employment services, skill development, social protection and social dialogue. It is necessary to enhance the capacity of agencies to formulate plans and policies for the future, taking into account the principles of the Employment Policy Convention, 1964 (No. 122), and the Employment Service Convention, 1948 (No. 88), both ratified by Thailand, as well as the Labour Administration Convention, 1978 (No. 150).

Discussions indicate that labour market information is sometimes understood to mean statistics rather than a broader concept that includes both qualitative information and quantitative data. These sources are complementary.

In addition to improved information, constituents have expressed a demand for improved capacity for better analysis of such information. Moreover, the demand for information extends beyond general profiles of the labour market to specific information on target groups in local areas, so that government agencies and workers' organizations can channel support to those people in need of assistance.

This chapter reviews existing systems and sources and makes recommendations for improving the quality and range of labour market information and enhancing the capacity to generate such information.

6.1 Users and producers

There currently exist many pieces of information on the labour market in various government agencies and private organizations. The challenge is to put them together in an effective, sustainable and affordable system that produces information useful in the analysis of labour market policies.

The .principal producers of labour market information are the Ministry of Labour and Social Welfare, the National Statistical Office, the Ministry of the Interior, the Office of the National Economic and Social Development Board and the Bank of Thailand. Various agencies produce statistics on education and training. Among these are the Ministry of Education and the Ministry of University Affairs. Other ministries supply additional information that is useful for examining labour issues in specific sectors of economic activity. Employers' organizations have contributed both data and analysis.[1] Research institutes and various NGOs have also played a role. The Thailand Development Research Institute Foundation compiles statistics and conducts research and analysis. Members of the Foundation have served on committees and acted as consultants for government agencies that are working on ways to improve their information systems.

Within the Ministry of Labour and Social Welfare there are several offices and various departments that collect and disseminate labour market information obtained from establishment surveys, administrative records and other sources. These include the Office of Social Security, the Department of Employment, the Department of Public Welfare, the Department of Skill Development and the Department of Labour Protection and Welfare. Each unit has responsibility for collecting and distributing data within its area of competence. In many respects this is a logical division of labour.

The National Statistical Office produces the Labour Force Surveys that are the principal source of regular and reliable labour statistics of comprehensive coverage. The main unit producing labour statistics in the National Statistical Office is the Social Statistics Division, which, in turn, has four branches: Population and Housing Statistics, Labour Force Statistics, Education and Social Statistics and the Social Research Branch. The Economics Statistics Division is responsible for several surveys including the Household Socio-economic Survey relating to household income and expenditure. The National Statistical Office is a user as well as a producer of labour market information. Insufficient recognition and support has been given to the Office's ongoing statistical programme that in many cases provides timely, comprehensive and reliable data for monitoring and evaluation.

The Ministry of the Interior is involved in collecting social statistics at the village level through its Department of Local Administration. The Human Resource Planning Division of the National Economic and Social Development Board collects data from various sources to produce indicators and undertake analysis. The Board's Development Evaluation Division has produced a series of reports on indicators of well-being and policy analysis with assistance from the Asian Development Bank for monitoring the impact of programmes and policies. Reports are disseminated through a series of newsletters. A pilot project is now underway in the Ministry of Industry to link information about the demand side by examining skill requirements in selected industries with information on the supply side from various ministries and training institutes. The Bank of Thailand disseminates macro-economic indicators and also collects a limited range of labour statistics.

---

[1] As a producer of information, ECONTHAI has provided the MOLSW with skill profiles to be used for training purposes. ECONTHAI has also produced estimates of the number of workers employed and the number of jobs lost by key sectors. See EIU. 1997. *Thailand, Business Operations Report 4th Quarter 1997*, Ch. 4: Labour, p. 16 (London).

6.2 Labour statistics: Sources, limitations and gaps

The principal sources of labour statistics are household-based censuses and surveys, establishment-based censuses and surveys, and administrative records and reports. Most social statistics from household units are from the population censuses, the Labour Force Surveys, the Socio-economic Surveys and the Village Census.

Basic demographic data have been obtained through the population censuses conducted by the National Statistical Office since 1960. In the *1990 Census of Population and Housing*, population data were produced by full enumeration, while other data covering areas such as employment and unemployment were collected on a sample basis. Demographic data are also available in administrative records.

The National Statistical Office has collected labour force statistics since 1963 in its Labour Force Survey. Beginning in 1971, two rounds of the survey were conducted each year: the first ran from January to March to coincide with the non-agricultural season, while the second ran from July to September during the agricultural season. After 1984, a third round was introduced in May. Requests for more frequent collection of data in response to the recent economic crisis prompted the introduction of a fourth round in November 1998. This was repeated in 1999 with funding from the Asian Development Bank. The quarterly surveys are now conducted in February (dry season), May (new graduates), August (wet season) and November (harvest period).

Even with quarterly data, an interpretation of changes must take into account the considerable seasonal variation in the labour force situation resulting from the agricultural production cycle. Working with the National Economic and Social Development Board, Kakwani has created indices that control for seasonal, structural, cyclical and random changes in employment, unemployment and real income.[2] However, many users do not readily understand the statistical methodology. The National Statistical Office has expressed an interest in introducing time series statistics with seasonally adjusted estimates that are straightforward and which can be readily understood by users.[3]

The Labour Force Surveys collect information on the *population* in and out of working age, defined as 13 years and above; the *working age population* by economic activity and age, sex, marital status, educational attainment and migration status; the *employed population* by age, sex, educational attainment, occupation, industry, status in employment, hours of work, income, fringe benefits and availability for additional work; and *unemployed persons* by duration of job search and type of previous work.

Survey content broadly follows international standards for the definitions and measurement of economic activity and related concepts. However, there are specific areas where clarification and changes might be useful. A number of proposals have been made on the questionnaire

---

[2] Nanak Kakwani. 1998. *Impact of the economic crisis on employment, unemployment and real income* (Bangkok, NESDB and ADB).

[3] Suggestions have been made by ILO/EASMAT to respond to this issue.

91

content and for improving the timeliness of the survey.[4] The National Statistical Office has recognized the need expressed by the National Economic and Social Development Board to re-engineer the Labour Force Survey through capacity building for statistical offices at the provincial level.[5] It has already introduced some of these measures. A preliminary report of the Labour Force Survey was released after two months and the final report was published within six months. Decentralization is in progress. While this may improve the speed of processing, it may have adverse affects on the quality of data. It involves strengthening the capacity of staff and procedures outside of Bangkok.

In trying to be more responsive to users, the National Statistical Office has added additional modules to the survey questionnaire. In February 1998, a special section was introduced, focusing on the economic crisis. Beginning in February 1999, a new module was added to examine social issues including training questions and another module for a study on home work.

The quality of provincial data is also under review. At present provincial estimates are not published in the *Report of the Labour Force Survey*. The planned redesign of the Labour Force Survey sample may improve precision of the estimates, but the quality of data processing still needs attention.

The Socio-economic Survey is a key source of information on household income, expenditure, assets and liabilities, housing characteristics and durable goods. The National Statistical Office has conducted the survey since 1957 and at two-year intervals beginning in 1988. The overall coverage and broad methodology are similar to the Labour Force Survey.

The Ministry of the Interior obtains information on employment as part of its Village Census.[6] While it is not designed to collect statistics, the census nevertheless produces data that are meant to be processed and tabulated to provide information in local communities and at higher levels. Due to a large volume of data being obtained by relatively inexperienced enumerators there is some concern as to whether the resulting statistics will be accurate and reliable. Questions have been raised about the methodologies used, and problems include aggregation in processing. There is also an issue of overlap and duplication with the Labour Force Survey. These data may add confusion regarding measurements of employment, unemployment and under-employment.[7]

---

[4] A SPPD project on Improvements in Policy Formulation through Improved Thailand Labour Force Surveys (THA/99/002/A/08/11, executed by the ILO and funded by the UNDP) addressed these issues. The major elements were: improved sampling schemes and introducing sample rotation; improving the speed and quality of data collection, processing and analysis; introducing a fourth survey round each year improving the content of the questionnaire and using supplementary modules on specific topics. Special modules for redundant workers, under-utilized labour and the informal sector could be used on a regular basis, while supplementary modules for specific topics such as school-leavers and child labour could be added on an annual basis or less frequently.

[5] NESDB. *National Paper 20*, for the Asian Regional Consultation on Follow-up to the World Summit for Social Development (Bangkok, 13-15 January 1999).

[6] This is the Social Welfare Promotion Project also known as the Village Welfare Assistance Project.

[7] The MOLSW also collects data from villages and the NSO conducts a village survey to update its sampling frame.

In response to requests for information growing out of the Asian financial crisis, the Asian Development Bank has funded a project to improve the Village Census. This is being implemented through the Department of Local Administration. Information is supposed to be made available at each level of government administration. The objective is to move beyond simply capturing local economic and social conditions, but also to obtain detailed information on target groups of displaced workers, unemployed persons and disadvantaged groups. At a grass roots level the Community Unemployment Register has been integrated into a structure that feeds information on open unemployment and "gross" underemployment[8] to an early warning system. Data collected by village committees and urban groups are passed on to the subdistrict, district, provincial and national levels.

Turning to establishment surveys, users have identified a number of problems with data generated. While recognizing the need for individual departments and agencies to produce appropriate information for administrative requirements, there is considerable scope for improving the coordination and rationalization of surveys. Suggestions from the ILO include maintaining a common business register, establishing a central focal point, improving sampling schemes, changing data content and consulting employers' groups.

The main source of administrative information on labour issues is the Ministry of Labour and Social Welfare, which collects and disseminates information on job applicants, job vacancies and job placements, working conditions, occupational safety and health, wages, hours of work and labour productivity. It is important that priorities be set for improvements in line with the ILO Labour Statistics Convention, 1985 (No. 160). Labour administrators and labour statisticians can then work together to suggest improvements in each of these priority areas, including procedures, forms, codes and processing of data.

A number of autonomous bodies and private organizations also compile labour market information. These include the National Productivity Institute, the Technological Promotion Association (Thai-Japan) and Thai Business Management Association.[9]

6.3 Key information on the labour market

6.3.1 Employment, unemployment and underemployment

One of the most controversial aspects of labour market information has been the widespread confusion resulting from different estimates for employment, unemployment and underemployment. In an effort to reduce the discrepancies in official statistics and to produce employment projections, the Committee on Labour Force, Employment and Unemployment Estimation has been established with the Department of Employment of the Ministry of Labour and Social Welfare serving as the secretariat. Among those serving on the Committee are the National Economic and Social Development Board, the National Statistical Office, the Bank of Thailand, the Thailand Development Research Institute and the Ministry of the Interior. In order to improve labour market analysis and produce labour force projections, a task force has

---

[8] The definition used does not follow international standards for time-related underemployment. Data are collected on employed persons working fewer than ten hours per week.

[9] Yongyuth Chalamwong; Sakdina Sontisakyotin; Napapan Meepadung. 1999. *Improvements in policy formulation through improved Thailand Labour Force Surveys*, Paper prepared for ILO/EASMAT (Bangkok, Human Resources and Social Development Programme, TDRI).

been assigned the role of overseeing the *Quarterly Labour Market Review* prepared by the Ministry of Labour and Social Welfare for the Council of Economic Ministers.

Conflicting data for measured unemployment result from different concepts used for definition and measurement. Some confusion also results from the seasonal nature of agricultural production. The Labour Force Survey collects data in respect of both "actual" and "usual" economic activity. The definitions used include the following:

Employed persons are defined as those 13 years of age and over who during the survey week, (1) worked for at least one hour for wages, profits, dividends or any other kind of payment, in kind; (2) did not work at all but had regular jobs, business enterprises or farms from which they were temporarily absent because of illness or injury, vacation or holiday, strike or lockout, bad weather, off-season or other reasons such as temporary closure of the workplace, whether or not they were paid by their employers during their period of absence, provided that in the case of a temporary closure of the workplace, the expectation was that it would be reopened within 30 days from the date of closure and they would be recalled to their former jobs; or (3) worked for at least one hour without pay in business enterprises or on farms owned or operated by household heads or members.

The unemployed include persons aged at least 13 years who during the survey period did not work for even one hour, had no jobs, business enterprises, or farms of their own, from which they were temporarily absent but were available for work. Unemployed persons in this category include (1) those who had been looking for work, during the preceding 30 days, and (2) those who had not been looking for work because of illness or belief that no suitable work was available, waiting to take up a new job, waiting for agricultural season or other reasons.[10]

While these are standard definitions useful for international comparisons, they have raised questions among data users following the current crisis. The criterion of working for one hour per week is confusing to users who are considering the issue of what it means to be unemployed and underemployed in a situation where most cannot afford to be out of work. Additional misunderstanding has resulted from the considerable variation in measured employment over the agricultural cycle. A farmer is classified as employed as long as there is a "regular job" in the agricultural sector, despite the fact that there may be no current work. Another issue relates to the comparability problems of using administrative records to estimate unemployment rates. The labour records provide data on registered job applicants. In a situation where the public employment exchange system is not comprehensively used, these data are generally not good proxies for unemployed persons.

The debate over concepts and methods of measurement is not unique to Thailand. However, recent frustration with conflicting figures during the economic crisis has led some critics to suggest that the Labour Force Survey be replaced or supplemented by other social statistics. Labour statisticians would point to the high standard of the Thai survey. Others would suggest more creative use of existing labour statistics, including different presentations and new tabulations together with improvements in the Labour Force Survey.

Establishment surveys are generally a principal source of employment statistics for the formal sector. Surveys conducted by the Ministry of Labour and Social Welfare and the

---

[10] NSO. 1998. *Report of the Labour Force Survey – Whole Kingdom, Round 3, August 1998*, pp. 41-42 (Bangkok).

National Statistical Office are currently not timely enough to provide useful signals for the labour market. There are also problems with the sampling frame, questionnaire design and response rate. The ILO has made suggestions to improve the system of surveys.

Supplementary estimates may also be compiled from the Social Security Fund records for employees covered by compensation insurance in all establishments employing ten or more workers and some smaller establishments. These records are reported on a monthly basis. Trends in the wage labour market are probably a fairly good proxy for trends in the general labour market. These data can be compared with those from the Labour Force Surveys to see how representative they may be in terms of employment trends. However, the fact that they cover only roughly one-fifth of the workers in Thailand is seen to be a shortcoming. An earlier ILO report also notes problems in using the data.[11] Among those not covered by the social security system are (i) government employees; (ii) employees of schools, universities and hospitals; (iii) daily paid temporary employees even if working in enterprises with 10 or more employees. This last exemption is a serious one, as these employees are likely to be the first to face layoffs. Thus, there are serious limitations, since data cover only part of the formal sector.

Through its Department of Employment, the Ministry of Labour and Social Welfare collects data on job seekers, job vacancies and job placements. Information for the supply side is derived from labour force registration of new entrants and retrenched workers. Data for the demand side are collected from its satellite employment offices and daily newspaper listings. This information suffers from difficulties encountered elsewhere regarding the small number and sample bias of those who report to employment exchanges. Job seekers do not generally register if the system does not provide an efficient mechanism to obtain job placements, and when there are not other incentives for registration such as receipt of benefits. Furthermore, few can afford the luxury of inactive unemployment. Some obtain employment through private agencies, newspaper listings and personal connections. Others go directly to the workplace. Many find jobs in self-employment in the informal sector. As a result of the crisis, the Department of Employment has established the Employment Service Operation Centre to work with both public and private employment services. It is not clear how far this service has been able to go in improving the situation or what kind of data will be produced.

It would be useful to have more information on the performance of Thailand's Public Employment Service. This would include the proportions of job seekers registered and placed by the employment services. In addition to these measures of *performance* it would be useful to have indicators of *quality* of services provided. This would require more information such as the speed of placement and the rate of retention of job seekers placed by the employment services. A recent study prepared for the ILO indicates that the placement to applicant ratio fell from about 67 per cent in 1997 to 53 per cent in 1998, while the placement to vacancies rate rose from around 60 percent to 80 per cent.[12] Additional information will be required if

---

[11] Pember. 1997. *Statistical monitoring of the labour market* (Bangkok, ILO/EASMAT, internal document).

[12] D. Fraser. 1999. *The role of employment services in the management of the Thai labour market: A study of the recent past and possibilities for commencing the twenty-first century*, Report prepared for the MOLSW (Bangkok, ILO/EASMAT, unpublished).

the receipt of unemployment insurance is conditional upon job search. Data related to opportunities for wage employment and self-employment should be linked to information for guidance, counselling and training. There is a need to improve the internal management information system and strengthen its access to labour market information and capacity for analysis.

Some of the debate about the usefulness of definitions for employment has pointed to the need for information about those who are employed but are inadequately employed in a number of ways. The most obvious is time-related underemployment for which International Conference of Labour Statisticians guidelines have now been established.[13] However, there are other forms of inadequate employment that, while difficult to measure, nonetheless represent important problems. One is the mismatch of skills represented by the educated unemployed. Another is the long hours and low income characteristic of many jobs in small enterprises and the informal sector.

6.3.2 Layoffs

The Ministry of Labour and Social Welfare collects and publishes data on layoffs. However, termination statistics are of limited usefulness due to the nature of coverage and the types of data. The Ministry compiles information about terminations of employment by industrial classification and by the three categories of production, service and administrative workers. It provides data for the numbers of establishments and employees and the reasons for termination. Focus group discussions conducted by the Brooker Group Consortium under the Asian Development Bank suggest that laid off-workers often go unreported to the Ministry, especially when employees are dismissed "step by step".[14] In addition to administrative records, survey data are also available for laid-off workers. The Labour Force Survey collects data on "former workers" by principal characteristics of the labour force. Specific questions are also asked about reasons for being unemployed.

Representatives of workers mention data on layoffs as a priority. Requests for information go beyond a profile of workers who have lost their jobs during the crisis. They are interested in learning more about who these workers are; where they are living; what they are doing; and what kind of assistance they need. These are the types of questions that are being asked as part of the Village Census conducted by the Department of Local Administration and are included in the early warning system of the Community Unemployment Register. In response to the crisis more detailed information on the urban unemployed will be collected by the Department of Employment of the Ministry of Labour and Social Welfare.

It has been suggested that follow-up studies be conducted to learn more about laid-off workers in terms of flows between unemployment and employment and between activity and inactivity. These could be broken down by age, sex, education, geographic location, migrant status and so forth to obtain a better understanding of target groups. More specifically, the study would find out whether laid-off workers find new jobs; the procedures they use for job searching; whether women find it more difficult than men to find new employment; and

---

[13] See the web site for the 16th International Conference of Labour Statisticians (Geneva, 1998) at http://www.ilo.org/public/english/120stat/res/underemp.htm.

[14] Narong Petprasert. 1998. *Study of the public response to the employment impact of the financial crisis in Thailand* (Bangkok, CPES, Chulalongkorn University).

whether women are more likely than men to drop out of the labour force. Technical assistance could be provided for a panel study, tracer survey or longitudinal survey.

6.3.3 Wages and earnings

It is not surprising that both employers' and workers' organizations mention wages as a priority for information. Employers have noted the need for better information on prevailing wages at the provincial level in view of the proposed decentralization of decision making regarding minimum wages. This issue is also tied to the use of foreign workers. Government agencies require better statistics for policy formulation. For example, the Department of Skill Development in the Ministry of Labour and Social Welfare needs wage data to promote skill development.

One of the results of the economic crisis is an increased demand for wage data on a timely basis. However, the available statistics collected through establishment surveys are not useful as "signals" due to lack of frequency and timeliness. The Department of Labour Protection and Welfare uses establishment surveys to collect wage data. Average wages are given for all employees. In addition there are breakdowns of the average wages of daily, monthly and piece-rate employees by industry, region and size of establishment. Wages are defined to include payment in cash and in kind for work during normal working hours or on a piece-rate basis including payments for work not done during holidays and leave. Earnings are defined as payments in cash and in kind for regular hours and overtime work together with allowances and bonuses such as cost-of-living allowances, meals, accommodation, travel, etc. The Ministry also compiles data on minimum wage rates.

The Labour Force Survey obtains information for total wage income, net business profits and net farm income, but there are doubts about the quality of this data especially for the self-employed. Household surveys rarely provide reliable measures of employment income. Total wage income is measured by wages and salaries, bonuses, overtime pay and other income. Data on wages and salaries are collected for all employees regardless of payment system and converted to monthly equivalents. Data are tabulated separately by sex, industry and occupation for government employees and the private sector. In addition to data on basic wages and salaries, information is also obtained regarding the receipt, but not the amounts, of supplementary benefits in cash and in kind. Cash supplements include payments for bonuses and overtime. Payments in kind include food, clothing, housing and transport.

Despite the fact that the Labour Force Survey is not the preferred method of collecting wage data, it has been used for this purpose in the absence of alternative sources that are available on a timely basis. Until better methods of collecting information on wages and earnings are identified, the usefulness of statistics from the Labour Force Survey could be assessed by making comparisons with data from the Socio-economic Survey for the same time periods. This would show users whether levels or trends of wage data and non-wage income can be used as indicators of conditions in labour markets.

6.4 Review of proposals for an improved system and capacity building

6.4.1 Challenges for a labour market information system

A labour market information system is basically a link between sources and uses of labour market information; it is a network of producers and users of both qualitative information and quantitative data. The functions of the system include collecting, processing, analysis and dissemination of labour market information. The quality of information may be assessed in terms of consistency, timeliness, continuity, transparency, accountability, relevance, accuracy, reliability, validity and accessibility. Attention should be paid to concepts and definitions, classifications and coding and presentation and dissemination.

An appropriate institutional framework is an essential part of a sustainable labour market information system. For some time, the users and producers of labour market information in Thailand have recognized the need for a system that would overcome some of the apparent problems with the existing mechanisms for producing information, formulating policies and monitoring programmes for the labour market.

(a) Communications and coordination

The present system lacks an effective and efficient mechanism for communications and coordination among producers and users of labour market information. This problem exists both within ministries and across agencies.

(b) Analysis and feedback

Despite improvements in labour market information and efforts to link producers and users through committees and seminars, the interactions between them are still inadequate. It is crucial that those who have made use of labour market information to identify issues, formulate policies and monitor programmes share their experiences, so that these lead to improvements in the system. Analysis and feedback should be part of each step in the process of finding adequate solutions to employment problems.

(c) Staff and expertise

Consultations with government agencies and research institutions have drawn attention to the importance of assigning staff and enhancing capacities for the collection, processing and analysis of labour market information. Within the Ministry of Labour and Social Welfare there is a need to identify staff who can take advantage of the training and experience being offered as part of programmes to improve the labour market information system.

(d) Fragmentation and overlap

There remains a substantial amount of fragmentation and overlap that could be reduced or eliminated through a coordinated system of information collection and data analysis. Following the financial crisis many users of statistical information have highlighted the need for reliable labour statistics that reflect current conditions and recent changes in the labour market. Many users have experienced concern and confusion when presented with statistics from different offices and departments. While government agencies do need to retain control and assume responsibility for their areas of competence, there must also be some degree of coordination in the distribution of information to users. A number of different committees and agencies have been established or suggested for this purpose. The Ministry of Labour and Social Welfare needs to choose a focal point to act as a coordinator. It would be useful for a single unit to be given the responsibility of analysing and reporting on trends in different segments of the labour market.[15]

---

[15] See Recommendations made by ILO/EASMAT in: ILO. 1994. *Improving labour and social statistics in Thailand*, A report submitted to the Government of Thailand (Bangkok, ILO/EASMAT); and Dipak Mazumdar. 1999. *Monitoring trends in the labour market*, Advisory paper prepared for the MOLSW (Bangkok, ILO/EASMAT).

(e)   Gaps in information

Several different "gaps" have been identified by users of labour market information. These include laid-off workers, underemployed workers, the educated unemployed, school leavers, wage rates and earnings data, the informal sector, micro-enterprises, labour mobility, labour demand, training statistics, child labour, illegal migrants and undocumented workers.[16] For the first time in many years, the educated unemployed represent a serious issue in public discussions. Ongoing debates regarding unemployment figures suggests that various measures of labour under-utilization be introduced and explained to both producers and users of information. Some of these gaps are being filled. However, analysts searching for information about labour market issues and particular target groups are not always aware of studies, research and reports. An efficient labour market information system can offer easier access to this information.

(f)   Techniques of collection

There is still room for improvement in the collection of labour statistics through the principal sources: household-based censuses and surveys, establishment censuses and surveys and administrative reports and records. A number of factors affect the quality of statistics, ranging from survey design to data dissemination. Among issues raised are outdated business registers, inadequately trained staff, under-reported earnings data, a lack of computer equipment, poor sample design, poorly designed questionnaires, frequent staff turnover, poor responses to business surveys and errors during entry and processing. The quality of statistics is also affected by the training of staff who produce and analyse labour market information. Although progress has been made there is still room for improvement, from field enumerators up to data analysts and policy makers.

6.4.2   Proposals for a labour market information system

A labour market information system should establish regular communication among producers and users of information. It is essential to have information units within agencies and a labour market information network among agencies. A number of suggestions have been made for a labour market information centre, including functions, structure, information, dissemination and location.

(a)   Functions

Various functions have been suggested for the focal point of the information system. These include compiling, updating, correcting and harmonizing data; linking information; conducting analysis; preparing reports; promoting brainstorming, feedback and ideas about labour market information; reviewing the system; co-ordinating linkages; creating consensus and organizing meetings, seminars and workshops. More specifically, a number of proposals have been made for the information centre. The 1994 ILO/EASMAT report on *Improving labour and social statistics in Thailand* suggests that a single unit should be responsible for a business register, establishment surveys, statistical standards, etc. Although the original proposal was that this should be within the Ministry of Labour and Social Welfare, the

---

[16] These were identified at the ILO Seminar on Improving the System of Labour Statistics in Thailand (Bangkok, 11 March 1998). In addition, participants mentioned industrial relations, work conditions and poverty issues.

ILO/EASMAT labour statistician has subsequently recommended that one agency should maintain a business register and that one *programme* should coordinate the establishment surveys.[17] A study prepared by the Thai Development Research Institute proposes a Human Resource Data Centre to collect information from various agencies, prepare reports on the labour market and provide an overview of the labour market information systems. The Centre would consist of an electronic link and a brainstorming forum for labour market information and a central commission of technical, statistical and manpower experts to update and correct information from various sources. The commission would be able to withstand pressures for political interference in the information system. The objectives are to collect, analyse and report information relating to the labour market. In addition to linking data among producing agencies, it is hoped that the centre will encourage efforts to coordinate information within agencies. An important function of the centre is to provide feedback in the form of ideas and opinions from users that will result in better information. Another alternative is the National Employment Management Information System conceptual framework proposed by the Brooker Group Consortium working under the Asian Development Bank technical assistance component on labour market enhancement. The National Employment Management Information System envisions a framework for (i) information gathering, coordination and analysis, (ii) policy advisory services and (iii) information dissemination and awareness building.

Thailand is ready to move beyond the production of statistics to a system of information related to labour markets. The exact functions of the labour market information system will depend upon political expediency as well as practical arrangements. It is recommended that the plan is considered carefully before it is implemented. At the beginning the list of functions should not be too ambitious.

(b) Structure

A question arising from earlier discussions about the information system concerns the nature of the link between users and producers of labour market information. A number of alternative structures have been proposed for the focal point or data centre for the labour market information system. One suggestion made by the ILO/EASMAT in 1994 for the Labour and Social Information Centre in the Ministry of Labour and Social Welfare includes sections for administration, information, computer systems, a library and services, statistical standards, maintenance of a business register and data collection and processing.[18] A report prepared for the Thai Development Research Institute for the Ministry's Department of Skill Development suggests a Human Resource Data Centre placed in the National Economic and Social Development Board with several agencies serving as "sub-centres". Finally, the National Employment Management Information System proposed under Asian Development Bank technical assistance envisions this as a top-level steering committee reporting to the Council of Economic Ministers. The National Economic and Social Development Board, the National Statistical Office and the Ministry of Labour and Social Welfare would provide advice to and receive suggestions from the National Employment Management Information System. Its operations would be linked to producers and users of labour market information.

---

[17] According to the ILO/EASMAT senior specialist in labour statistics, there are reasons to place the register and surveys within the NSO.

[18] The first four components are part of MOLSW Order No. 3/1994 and the last three sections are suggested in the 1994 ILO/EASMAT report.

(c)   Scope of information to be collected

Another issue raised in discussions about the labour market information system is the scope of data that are collected. Should information cover labour markets narrowly defined, or should it deal with human resources from a broader perspective? Should it include other social information? Are economic statistics to be part of the data system? The types of information should be determined by users in both government agencies and the private sector. A suggested framework is given in Annex A.

The construction and maintenance of a labour market information system is a very resource-intensive endeavour. Decisions need to be made about which links should be established between existing databases, what information should be "harmonized" in a common database, what kinds of publications, files, bibliographies and references should be held at the centre, etc. In the process it is important that there be serious consultations between users and producers of data.[19]

(d)   Dissemination

Dissemination as one of the functions of a labour market information system has already been mentioned. Two points might be added. First, many agencies in the government have already constructed web sites that either provide data directly to users or give information about the availability of data in other formats. Web sites also contain hyperlinks that connect various sources of labour market information. These networks already serve as a method of dissemination. Second, it is proposed that the *Quarterly Labour Market Review* currently prepared by the Committee on Labour Force, Employment and Unemployment Estimation be expanded into a periodic newsletter. This will require support and supervision by a unit rather than a committee.

(e)   Location

Although a focal point for an information centre has been under discussion for some time, no agency has stepped forward to take up the role. One explanation is that lead agencies are "not ready". Several suggestions have been made, including the selection of the Ministry of Labour and Social Welfare, the National Statistical Office, the National Economic and Social Development Board and the Thai Development Research Institute.[20]

6.5 Policy recommendations

Points raised in this chapter were discussed during the national Tripartite Consultation on Labour Market Information Systems in Thailand in Bangkok on 21 July 1999. On the basis of this discussion, an attempt was made to identify priorities. Two sets of recommendations are

---

[19] Preliminary lists of suggested data have already been prepared by ILO/EASMAT and the TDRI. ILO. 1994. *Improving labour and social statistics in Thailand*, Report submitted to the Government of Thailand (Bangkok, ILO/EASMAT); and Niphon Phuaphongsakon and Yaowarat Sirwaranan. 1998. *Human Resource Data Centre Study, Supporting Document Set 8, A Study for the purpose of preparing the Human Resource Development Master Plan of Thailand B.E. 2504-2549*, prepared for the Department of Skills Development, MOLSW (Bangkok, TDRI, unofficial English translation by ILO/EASMAT).

[20] A number of issues were raised during discussions about the TDRI proposal by Niphon Phuaphongsakon and Yaowarat Sirwaranan. op. cit.

proposed. The first relate to improving the range and quality of labour market information, while the second focuses on enhancing capacity for analysis.

6.5.1 Improved quality, consistency and coordination of labour market information

The following steps should be accorded a high priority.

(a) Establish a working group to decide on a focal point for a national labour market information system

Consideration should be given to the functions, structure and location for the labour market information system centre or focal point. Attention was drawn earlier to proposed options and substantial feedback on these issues. In order to decide on a permanent focal point for labour market information, it is recommended that a working group be established with employers' groups, workers' organizations, the Ministry of Labour and Social Welfare, the National Statistical Office, the National Economic and Social Development Board and the Thai Development Research Institute as leading members. The ILO could serve as an interested observer and provide technical support. In the meantime, the Committee for Labour Force, Employment and Unemployment Estimation would serve a coordinating role for disseminating statistics and preparing reports on the labour market with the Department of Employment in the aforementioned Ministry.

(b) Expand ongoing efforts to improve labour statistics

Efforts should continue to improve the compilation of data from household-based surveys, establishment surveys and administrative records as suggested earlier. These will serve to strengthen labour market information on the formal sector. In addition it is proposed that an informal sector survey be introduced, including:

(i) *Labour force survey:* Improvements are currently being implemented with assistance from the UNDP.

(ii) *Establishment-based surveys:* The existing programme of establishment-based surveys should be improved by creating and maintaining a central register of businesses, using sampling schemes and introducing sample rotation, improving the content of questionnaires and minimizing duplication of surveys. The ILO has proposed guidelines for concepts, coverage and frequency of surveys.[21] It is urgent that these recommendations are reviewed and decisions taken to implement changes, so that these surveys can be put on a firm basis. It is suggested that the National Statistical Office be responsible for the implementation of surveys. The content and design should be coordinated with various departments of the Ministry of Labour and Social Welfare.

(iii) *Labour statistics based on administrative records:* Modifications might begin with forms and procedures for reporting. Subsequently, the data need to be coded and processed so that relevant statistics can be exported from the administrative database. Implementing the proposed changes may require provisions for computer equipment and staff training. The ILO/EASMAT publication, *Labour statistics based on administrative records: Guidelines on compilation and presentation* (Bangkok, 1997), which has been translated into Thai,

---

[21] Robert Pember. 1998. *Improvements to the system of establishment-based surveys in Thailand* (Bangkok, ILO/EASMAT, internal document).

provides detailed guidelines for this purpose. Within the Ministry of Labour and Social Welfare, priority areas should include data from public employment services and the Social Security Office. *Informal sector survey:* Along with improvements in data collection for the formal sector, priority attention should be devoted to improving the knowledge base on the informal sector, which accounts for the bulk of the employed labour force. Improvements introduced to the Labour Force Survey now provide better information on employment in the informal sector. The National Statistical Office has conducted studies of small and medium-sized enterprises in collaboration with the Ministry of Labour and Social Welfare. However, it is recommended that an informal sector survey be conducted that would provide detailed information on the sector for policy makers. The recommendation made in Chapter 2 for an informal sector survey should, therefore, receive high priority.

(c) *Develop key labour market indicators*

While recent focus has been on the unemployment rate, a broader set of core indicators is essential for active labour market policies. It is suggested that the principal users of labour market information identify a key set of labour market indicators. Consultations with social partners indicate the following to be high priorities: labour slack; informal sector and micro-enterprises; income from employment; productivity and costs; internal migration; and target groups. Wherever information is collected about the characteristics of the population, the data should be broken down by sex. In addition, data should be classified by age groups to show the position of children, youth and adults. Most of the data needed for the indicators are already available from the Labour Force Survey and labour administration records (see Annex A).

(d) *Improve labour market information for local level policies*

In accordance with the Eighth National Economic and Social Development Plan and the Thailand Social Policy Committee initiatives, there is increased emphasis on decentralization, community development and local planning. This requires detailed information at provincial, district or village levels which can be used to identify target areas and target groups when planning special development and employment projects and programmes. Local administrators also need this information to monitor and evaluate projects.

Two initiatives in this direction have already been highlighted: improvements in the Labour Force Survey data collected at the provincial level, and information collected at the village level by the Department of Local Administration of the Ministry of the Interior and the Ministry of Labour and Social Welfare. The different objectives, strengths and weaknesses of the two methods and their complementary nature should be recognized. These two approaches should not compete for funds and recognition. An efficient labour market information system could improve cooperation and coordination among the agencies involved in these projects. It is suggested that links be established at a local level on a pilot basis between labour market information and other social statistics obtained from the Community Unemployment Register and the Labour Force Survey.

6.5.2 Enhanced capacity for labour market analysis to design, implement and monitor active labour market policies

Enhancing of the capacity of government agencies and social partners to analyse, interpret and use labour market information was identified by the July 1999 Tripartite Consultation held in Bangkok as the second area of priority. A number of steps need to be taken – some need immediate attention, while others are longer-term. The proposals made here pertain mainly to building the capacity of the Ministry of Labour and Social Welfare.

(a) Establish a technical unit for compilation and analysis of labour market information within the Ministry of Labour and Social Welfare

Within the Ministry of Labour and Social Welfare it is suggested that a technical unit be established to analyse and report on trends in different segments of the labour market [Mazumdar, 1999]. The unit might be divided into branches, one using data from the Labour Force Survey and Socio-economic Survey covering the whole economy including the informal sector, and another dealing specifically with the formal sector. It would serve as a coordinating unit and replace the fragmented system that now exists with technical studies and planning units in each department. The unit should be comprised of staff with competence in labour economics, quantitative research, statistical analysis and information technology. It should be responsible for producing the *Quarterly Labour Market Review* and carry out studies on topical labour and employment issues. It could also commission specific studies and surveys from suitable agencies on selected topics. Collaborative projects with outside experts would serve to enhance in-house capacity at the beginning.

(b) Support priority programmes of technical assistance for capacity enhancement

The enhancement of capacity within the Ministry of Labour and Social Welfare for policy formulation and labour market analysis cannot be accomplished overnight. It will require a major programme of technical assistance. The ILO has proposed a project for Capacity Enhancement for Labour Market Monitoring, Analysis and Policy Formulation for this purpose. The project aims at enhancing the capacity of offices and departments within the Ministry to conduct policy-oriented analysis on crucial labour issues. It also supports improvements of labour market indicators and signals for the formal and informal sectors and short-term forecasting. It is recommended that the Ministry should seek funding for this project and implement it as soon as possible.

Annex A

Suggested Framework for Selection of Labour Market Indicators[22]

1. Employment and Work (Labour Utilization)

- Labour force participation rates
- Inactivity rates
- Employment to population ratio
- Normal working hours per week
- Actual working hours per week
- Annual working hours
- Full-time and part-time work

2. Unemployment and Underemployment (Labour Under-utilization)

- Unemployment rate
- Long-term unemployment rate
- Inactivity rate
- Duration of unemployment
- Ratio of female to male unemployment rate
- Ratio of youth to adult unemployment rate
- Discouraged worker rate
- Registered unemployment for youth
- Time-related underemployment
- Real earnings per worker

3. Structure of Employment (Labour Market Structure)

Traditional indicators:

- Industry
- Status in employment
- Occupation
- Institutional sector (government, parastatal and private)

Other indicators:

- Informal sector
- Establishment size
- Export orientation

4. Skill Level of the Labour Force

- Educational attainment of employed population (proportion of employed population with primary, secondary and tertiary education)

---

[22] This framework draws on a classification developed by Richard Anker of ILO, Geneva, for Key Indicators of the Labour Market.

- Percentage of labour force receiving technical education and VT
- Proportion of youth cohort in pre-employment training and apprenticeship
- Professional and technical workers as a proportion of total employment

Other measures could be used as proxy variables for the labour force:

- Intake rates, transition rates, enrolment ratios, completion rates and dropout rates
- Qualifications of educators and trainers
- Teacher to student ratios
- Literacy/illiteracy rates
- Percentage of youth cohort graduating in engineering and sciences
- Public expenditure on education and training
- Percentage of total education budget spent on technical education and VT
- Expenditure per student

5. Labour Exchange Functions

- Job applicants, vacancies and placements (stocks and flows)
- Percentage of applicants placed
- Vacancies per applicant
- Vacancies filled per vacancies received
- Terminations of employment
- Duration of unemployment
- Length of time to fill a vacancy
- Percentage of vacancies notified to the employment services
- Percentage of unemployed job seekers as a percentage of total unemployed persons
- Number of foreigners applying for work permits
- Number of nationals working aboard

6. Worker and Employer Cooperation

- Percentage of labour force covered by collective agreements
- Proportion of labour force in unions

7. Labour Costs and Productivity

- Labour costs
- Compensation of employees
- International unit labour costs
- Productivity indices
- Producer price indices
- Wage-productivity gap

8. Workers' Pay and Income

- Average wages and salaries
- Average wage of unskilled workers at entry level
- Female wages as a percentage of male wages
- Statutory minimum wage
- Real earnings per worker

9. Job Quality and Employment Security

- Percent of employees with a contract
- Type of contract (e.g. per cent with temporary and casual work agreement)
- Proportion of workers with multiple activities (e.g. at school and at work)
- Percentage of employed persons with multiple jobs
- Proportion of employed persons covered by social security
- Occupational injuries, illness and deaths (work accident rate, deaths due to work accidents, number of days lost through accidents)
- Average days of annual holidays
- Labour turnover (job stability and job changes)
- Labour transitions (employment/unemployment/inactivity and school to work)

10. Selected Supplementary Competitiveness Indicators

- Value of manufacturing exports as a percentage of GDP
- Major exports by commodity groups
- Percentage distribution of manufacturing exports by technological category
- Foreign direct investment as a percentage of gross domestic fixed capital Formation
- R&D Employment and Expenditures
- ISO Certificates

11. Poverty and Inequality

- Gini coefficients
- Shares of income by quintile
- Percentages of the population below national and international poverty lines

12. Ratification of Fundamental ILO Conventions

Chapter 7
Conclusions and Recommendations

In mid 1997, Thailand's economy, and by extension its processes of economic and social policy-making, suffered a severe and dislocating shock. The global economy, which had done so much to raise standards of living and which had guided so much investment and shaped the country's economic structure, proved an unreliable partner. Growth and structural change went into reverse gear. Prices fell and debts could not be repaid; workers were laid off and many returned to villages; construction sites were abandoned and surplus capacity emerged in industry. The recovery process has been slow, partly because of a reluctance to lend on the part of commercial banks and partly because of poor investment prospects. However, recovery is being aided by a large fiscal deficit, financed partly by concessional loans from abroad, which is used to promote a wide range of income- and employment-generating programmes. There has been a real devaluation but not, however, a very major one. Markets fairly quickly pushed the baht up from its lowest nominal point. As a result of the relatively small real devaluation and of the extent of recession in the region as a whole the external sector has not helped in Thailand's recovery as much as might have been expected. Similarly the relatively small real devaluation does little to change the relative price structure facing Thailand in terms of export and import prices. However, wages in US dollar terms are low (after a major fall in per capita GDP of around 12 per cent) so that temporarily the pressure to upgrade less profitable and labour-intensive production processes in exporting is relaxed. However, this relief cannot last more than three or four years.

In terms of the objective of full employment and decent jobs for all, which the ILO is committed to promoting and which Thailand has endorsed both through the World Summit for Social Development held in Copenhagen in 1995 and the ILO Declaration on Fundamental Principles and Rights at Work, there are perhaps three lessons to be learnt from the crisis:

(i)   That such a dislocation should not be allowed to recur;

(ii)   That future growth must be sustainable;

(iii)   That the pattern of growth, or at least its outcomes in terms of income distribution and access to income and jobs, should be more equitable (see Chapter 1.1.6 a).

The first point, that such a crisis should not be allowed to recur, is one that has implications for domestic economic policy making and, of course, for the international community overall. No political or social system, of course, can by its processes and procedures give a guarantee that only good economic policies and decisions are made. However, encouraging debate on economic issues as well as pluralism in the institutions which are well informed on economic problems widens the range of options for decision taking.

A fully fledged tripartite machinery might well have given other suggestions on aspects of economic and financial policy which, if adopted, could have reduced the danger of disruption stemming from excessive reliance on short-term capital flows (see Chapter 1).

The second point relates to the sustainability of growth. This effectively concerns the ability of the economic system to move relatively smoothly into new and higher value-added activities and allocate resources accordingly. There are many preconditions to be met for this process to operate effectively. One of these is to achieve a high level of capital investment, which requires the interaction of foreign and domestic business interests and government. Judicious investment by small enterprises which enables them to expand their range and scale of operations is particularly important. One contention of this report is that the sustainability of Thailand's pre-crisis growth was already under threat. The relatively low skill level of the labour force was obstructing the shift from labour-intensive export production into more technologically sophisticated activities. At the same time real producer wages were outstripping labour productivity in the manufacturing sector in general. In the 1990s, labour productivity growth in manufacturing was lower than the average for the whole economy, which suggests a persistence of labour intensive activities. The direction of causality is, however, unlikely to be established unequivocally. Arguments for pointing a finger at a skills deficit are the relatively low average education level of the labour force and the apparently rudimentary level of training given both in government institutions and on the job (see Chapter 4). The first of these is changing relatively rapidly, aided by the fall in the share of unpaid family workers in the labour force as the latter becomes dominated by wage employment (see Chapter 1). Thailand is currently experiencing a period of fast expansion of education at the upper secondary and tertiary level but inevitably the quality of the teaching staff needs much improvement.

The third point concerns the distribution of income and equity in access to jobs and income. Thailand has long had a more unequal distribution of household income than is common in the Asian region, partly associated with marked disparities in incomes and poverty in different regions of the country. The spread of wage earning, however, is a feature associated with growing income equality. A good supply of skilled, or trainable, workers is, however, likely to be needed if skill differentials are not to lead to a growing inequality in wage incomes. Similarly, tertiary education needs to be of good quality throughout. Equality of access is also affected by regional features influencing, for example, school enrolment, teaching quality and dropout rates. In terms of equality of access to jobs and incomes, progress towards gender equality is being made, particularly in access to education and in the labour legislative field. However women are poorly represented in skilled jobs and at the managerial levels, over-represented in repetitive jobs in manufacturing for export and in low-quality, low-income work in the informal sector, and notoriously liable to exploitation in the commercial sex sector. Migrant labour in Thailand faces additional problems of discrimination. A further issue concerns conditions of work in the small-scale and informal sector. Workers in small, and particularly small and unregistered – or informal – enterprises, can respond to the crisis only by seeking to supplement their often reduced earnings. They may, of course, work longer hours in the same job. It is important to put the enterprises in which they work on a stronger footing, upgrade their technology where possible and enhance the availability of credit and finance.

The financial crisis, of course, showed up many problems of a social nature where institutional mechanisms were weak. These have largely concerned income-compensation and employment-generating programmes. Before the crisis only a limited scheme of severance pay was in existence and no system of unemployment benefit applied. For many workers and their families, health care benefits depended on formal employment. With the crisis, a large number of jobs disappeared but few of the workers affected received any form of income compensation. Underemployment increased, as did unemployment (although not so spectacularly as in the Republic of Korea) and, especially with the arrival of outside finance, plans for labour-intensive public works programmes were taken down from the shelves. There would appear, however, to have been many problems in their targeting and implementation. While the public employment service had a major role to play, its operation can be improved.

In addition, the crisis put a strain on tripartite relations. In Thailand, neither workers nor employers are well organized and collective bargaining is little advanced. Enterprise level social dialogue apparently helped to ease or make more orderly the processes of retrenchment and short-time working. There are also incipient tripartite processes and mechanisms at the national level, dealing, among other things, with minimum wage fixing, which are likely to gain in importance in the future. But there are problems with deficiencies in legislation and the proper framework for tripartism is not yet at hand.

The recommendations made in this study have the intention of shaping labour market institutions and practices, if necessary through legislation, to serve the three objectives mentioned earlier of avoiding a repetition of the crisis, securing sustainable growth and moving towards more equal outcomes of the growth process together with achieving non-discrimination and greater equality of access to jobs and incomes. Recommendations are made in the following areas: small-scale enterprise development, employment-generating schemes, public employment services, minimum wage policy, social protection, skill development, social dialogue, labour market information and gender equality at work.

7.1 Gender equality at work

Progress has been made in adopting policies and legislation to promote equality of opportunity and treatment between male and female workers. However, in order to provide decent work for men and women in reality, Thailand's major programmes in the labour and social protection fields should be made more sensitive and responsive to gender concerns. The capacity of ILO constituents needs to be enhanced to ensure that these programmes benefit women and men equally and to enable the successful design, adoption, management and evaluation of special measures in fields where pronounced gender inequalities are known to exist, or in sectors or areas where many vulnerable girls and women are found.

Since the late 1990s, girls and boys have had almost equal educational opportunities at the primary, secondary and tertiary levels. Girls and women, however, should receive more equal access to training, business support services and credit, and women's participation in decision making should increase. Integrated packages of support services geared towards their economic and social empowerment are needed for those women workers with little education and few skills who have been retrenched, and for home-workers who find themselves at the end of the subcontracting chain beyond labour protection and with little bargaining power. More generally, the recent increase in poverty has jeopardized earlier gains made in the more equal distribution of resources among the population, and women from poor population groups especially need to gain access to productive employment and social protection alongside their male counterparts. All critical employment and labour data for policy makers should be disaggregated by sex so that conclusions for policy and action are drawn from an awareness of gender differentials in employment and income.

The commercial sexual exploitation and trafficking of children and women are subjects of grave concern in the country. The emphasis is on the prevention of such abuses and the withdrawal and rehabilitation of the victims. Building on the experience gained so far, especially in Thailand, future action by governmental and non-governmental organizations, the ILO and other international organizations will focus on the expansion of successful strategies geared towards capacity building of said organizations at the subregional, national and local levels, and on direct action in communities to provide alternative livelihoods to those at risk. Providing more adequate services to the children and women who have been trafficked across borders is a challenge which will receive priority attention.

7.2 Small enterprise development

There is a need to create a policy framework that provides the necessary motivation, and direction for strengthening and expanding the micro-, small and medium-sized enterprises and for raising productivity. In terms of overall policy, there should be a shift in emphasis away from financial support to help in business development services, particularly through private sector service providers – especially small-scale providers. Greater attention should be devoted to improving the employment- and income-generating potential of the service and trade sectors, in addition to the current emphasis on manufacturing industries. The Government should develop greater coordination among those promoting enterprise development, including economic and non-economic ministries, the private sector and the NGO community. The Ministry of Labour and Social Welfare and the Community Development Department of the Ministry of the Interior should be included in new institutions such as the Institute for Small and Medium Enterprise Development. Private sector representation could be widened by involving associations of small-scale entrepreneurs.

Greater emphasis on support for micro-enterprises is needed. They have been denied support and recognition by the economic line ministries, and must rely on the welfare-oriented support services of the social ministries. Member-based associations of micro- and small-scale entrepreneurs should be encouraged and institution-building programmes should be provided in order to develop their capacity to provide services to their members. Support policies that could increase the graduation rate from informal to formal enterprises will have a significant impact given the existence of large numbers of micro-enterprises.

A new study of the informal sector is needed to highlight the profile and constraints on male and female workers. This would enable policy makers to identify ways to design more effective policies and support programmes for the sector as well as to encourage decent work through better working conditions. Given inadequate information about economic, working and social conditions or access to productive and financial resources of the large number of women engaged in the informal sector and micro-enterprises, it is recommended that an in-depth study be carried out to identify the barriers and constraints they face. The study could also indicate ways in which working conditions, health and safety can be improved.

7.3 Employment generating schemes

Programmes of social investment have to fit into a longer-term strategy for employment and growth. This should be in line with the Eighth Plan objectives of people's empowerment and decentralization. To enable communities to respond effectively several steps are necessary. These include: improved information collection at the local level through coordination of efforts such as the Community Unemployment Register, the Unemployed Graduates Programme and Village Welfare Centres; links between different employment- and income-generation programmes at the local level to avoid overlapping and duplication; skills and management training of community leaders and target groups; participatory approaches; self-employment through community-based micro-credit schemes; and targeted programmes to address the special problems of home workers, retrenched women workers, girls and women prone to becoming involved in the sex trade or other types of labour exploitation, and girls and women rescued from such abusive work.

Implementing agencies need training in project preparation, appraisal and management. Both public sector agencies and private agencies need orientation in incorporating labour-based, appropriate technology approaches in infrastructure investment programmes for their employment potential to be realized. Project monitoring and evaluation is generally a weak area where international agencies can assist.

Employers' and workers' organizations need to be involved in social investment and job creation programmes. At present, these are mainly implemented by government line agencies, NGO networks and community-based organizations. It will be useful to involve representatives of workers and employers in identifying target groups, developing projects and programme monitoring.

7.4 Public employment services

It is important to make the public employment service more effective, especially in a period of job scarcity. Management capacity may be improved through using relevant performance indicators. The capacity of employment services staff in the use of all sources of labour market information and data and their analysis and interpretation should be increased in order to follow trends in local and regional labour markets as a supplement to their administrative data. Labour exchange and other information on employment services' activities should be disseminated to job seekers and employers through the Internet.

It is also important to develop the capacity of the Public Employment Service to plan, monitor and evaluate the labour market adjustment programmes it administers (e.g. training, retraining and job creation programmes).

The Service should strive for an optimal balance between labour exchange services to general job seekers (through the recent development of job seekers and vacancies banks on computer terminals and the Internet) and more focused and intensive job search assistance to disadvantaged groups (e.g. the long-term unemployed, unemployed youth and disabled persons).

As the Government of Thailand is studying the possible introduction of an unemployment insurance scheme, a thorough review of the policy and organization of unemployment insurance with a special focus on the role of employment services should be undertaken.

7.5 Minimum wages

Although a decision has been taken to decentralize the minimum wage, there is inadequate information on the pros and cons of this measure. This should be taken up for further study in Phase II of the ILO/Ministry of Labour and Social Welfare study on wage policy and labour competitiveness.

There has been a high degree of compliance with the minimum wage in Thailand. With the suspension of the active minimum wage policy after the crisis, it is all the more important to protect workers' wages at the lower end of the wage scale by ensuring continued high compliance.

There is a tendency for enterprise pay structures to be based on the minimum wage with pronounced compression of wage scales. Employers should instead pay wages above the minimum, based on performance and skills. This will provide incentives to workers to acquire skills.

7.6 Social protection

There are policy issues to be resolved in respect of the partially funded social insurance pension approach adopted by the Social Security Office, and the strategy of the Ministry of Finance for the integration of fully funded pension and provident funds into one system under an institution linked to private sector fund management. The defined benefit principle and partial funding system would seem to be the most appropriate forms for the public pension scheme to be implemented by the Social Security Office.

There is no specific institutional mechanism to oversee policy formulation and coordination over the entire field of social protection, including social insurance and social assistance polices. The overall coordination authority might be vested in the Ministry of Labour and Social Welfare in view of its extensive and vested responsibilities for social protection, with the collaboration of the Ministries of Finance and Public Health.

The Social Security Office might usefully establish clear strategic objectives and work plans in respect of: (i) the extension of coverage to workers of small-size enterprises employing less than ten workers and in the rural and informal sectors, including possible support through micro-insurance schemes and community-based schemes; (ii) the assessment of a possible extension of health care coverage; and (iii) the improvement of the old-age and workmen's compensation pension schemes in line with relevant ILO standards and to ensure long-term financial viability.

The 1998 ILO study on the assessment of the introduction of unemployment insurance in Thailand recommended that unemployment insurance be introduced with a target date of 2001 provided that the decision-making and administrative process would be initiated at that time. While there are obvious differences of opinion among social partners on the timing of the scheme, the Government might wish to consider deciding in principle to introduce unemployment insurance and starting the technical and administrative preparatory processes immediately, as recommended in the ILO study. The Government might also consider undertaking a thorough review of the policy and organization of unemployment insurance, focusing especially on its administrative infrastructure and integration with the Public Employment Service. The unemployment insurance system should only be put in place if integrated with employment services for the two key purposes of reporting, and taking active labour market measures for reintroducing the unemployed into the workforce.

The Social Security Office should become an independent agency under the Ministry of Labour and Social Welfare and be freed from civil service staffing constraints in order to increase its capacity to play the central role in an extended system of social protection.

7.7 Skills development

While the development of a new Vocational Education and Training Act will provide the legal basis for the reform of the technical and vocational education system, it is essential that a broad-ranging national vocational training strategy should be developed. The strategy should provide guidance on areas of responsibility and identify a framework for coordination between training providers. It should also provide guidance on questions of access and equity, the role of the private sector and the financing of vocational education and training, as well as addressing the structural and legislative changes necessary to expand and improve the quality of skill training.

The lack of an effective and modern national system of skill recognition is a major constraint to developing a skilled workforce. Many countries in the region have followed the global trend to competency-based systems of skill recognition linked to clearly identified industrial competencies.

The new Education Act will concentrate on expanding and improving the quality of the present education system. Those presently in the workforce will require a different approach. A concerted national campaign to improve the general education skills of workers who were not able to continue at school should be a high priority for both the Government and enterprises.

It is increasingly recognised that a gender-differentiated approach to education and training policies needs to be taken. In Thailand, girls and women need to be encouraged to enrol in technical and vocational education and vocational training, especially in fields which lead to productive employment and they must be provided with a safe training environment that is free from sexual harassment. Quality training needs to be combined with the provision of credit and business support services to particularly vulnerable groups of women, such as retrenched, uneducated and older women, as well as women who are either at risk of becoming part of the commercial sex industry, or want to leave it or have already left.

Small enterprises often lack resources or facilities to provide training. Furthermore, training institutions have not attempted to target small enterprises by providing them with the kind of training and flexibility needed. Attention has to focus on establishing networks or sectoral clusters of firms which can improve access to training for small enterprises.

The Department of Vocational Education's Dual Vocational Training project appears to be a promising source of skilled workers. There are very few other long-term skilled worker training programmes which combine industrial and institutional training components. However, the programme would need to be expanded considerably if it is to have a significant impact at the national level.

In a similar manner, the pre-employment programmes of the Department for Skill Development could be modified and expanded into a national apprentice system, with alternating periods of enterprise- and institution-based training. The existing courses already have an attachment to enterprises as a component.

In order to promote training at the enterprise level, several steps are necessary: the establishment of selected industry-based training centres; the deregulation of training provisions; the expansion of tax and financial incentives for training; the expansion of accreditation and registration of private training providers; and the piloting of public-private partnerships in training.

7.8 Social dialogue

Social dialogue relies on the strength of the parties involved. In Thailand, therefore, there is a need to overcome the dual problems of under-representation and fragmented interests through the following policy priorities.

Freedom of association is guaranteed in Thailand's new Constitution. The ratification of the ILO's main Conventions on this, the Freedom of Association and Right to Organize Convention, 1948 (No. 87), and the Right to Organize and Collective Bargaining Convention, 1949 (No. 98), should be a subject for immediate consideration, especially as the country's main labour relations laws have either undergone or are currently under review. Certain ongoing efforts to achieve legislative change resulted in the passage of the State Enterprise Labour Relations Act in 2000 which has removed constraints on trade union formation and collective bargaining in state-owned enterprises. However, there is still a need to provide stronger protection against the victimization of labour organizers in the private sector. Also, the excessive fragmentation of the labour movement renders it difficult for labour to speak with a unified voice. The Government needs to rethink the criteria on which labour federations are legally formed with a view to encouraging the formation of larger, more comprehensive labour federations. It should remove the incentive to fragmentation that currently exists through the one union/one vote system of apportioning labour seats on tripartite bodies. Law should place no prohibition on trade unions in the public and private sectors becoming affiliates of the same labour federation. As for employers' organizations, the law needs to allow individual enterprises to become full members of the peak employers' organizations. Registration of employers' organizations needs to be rationalized within one ministry, not several.

Strengthening bipartism should also be a priority. The draft of the reform Labour Relations Act on which the Ministry of Labour and Social Welfare is currently working would mandate the creation of labour-management councils in enterprises employing more than 15 persons. This is a positive step. The law needs to ensure the transparency of election criteria and the protection of employee representatives in their function and in their freedom of speech and action. The law needs to ensure that the role of trade unions and collective bargaining at the enterprise level is protected in the functioning of the labour-management councils. The law also needs to be reformed to reduce constraints on collective bargaining and the right to strike. The legal use of the strike when bargaining comes to an impasse is too restricted. The list of essential services and other industries in which the legal strike is curtailed is excessively long. The law also needs to remove other criteria, such as the "state of the economy", as a legitimate reason for limiting collective bargaining.

The other major area of attention should be the strengthening of tripartism. Unequal representation means that the Government voice dominates at the expense of workers and employers. There needs to be better representational balance in the tripartite bodies. The scope, the mandate and the authority of Thailand's tripartite mechanisms need to be clarified and reinforced in order to increase their credibility and effectiveness. The criteria for appointment to tripartite mechanisms need to be transparent and to be based on the true representativeness of organizations, and on the knowledge and competence of the participants in the subject matter. As a means of redressing part of the shortfall in competence, the Government needs a formal training policy for participants in tripartite bodies. Training should focus on the substance of the issues dealt with (e.g. wage-fixing) but also on skills for tripartite decision-making. Finally, the range of subjects currently discussed in tripartite bodies needs review. For example, there is currently no tripartite mechanism wholly devoted to employment policy. Filling this gap would foster dialogue on productivity improvement and training needs.

Social dialogue might usefully expand beyond tripartite representatives. Tripartism can be strengthened if representatives are allowed to have recourse to experts in their deliberations.

Improving the knowledge of the role of workers' and employers' organizations and social dialogue is also important. There is a need – irrespective of policy reform – for the trade unions and employers' organizations themselves to advance their own cause in a more effective way and attempt to overcome their representation and fragmentation problems. Trade unions could be strengthened if they were financially sound. Thought should be given to criteria for a "dues checkoff" system at the workplace. There is a general need to improve knowledge of legal rights and the functions of labour market institutions. A modest (and low cost) proposal to fill this gap would be for the Government simply to launch a media campaign through which knowledge of laws and rights is diffused, and the role of workers' and employers' organizations, as well as that of collective bargaining, are clearly expressed as public policy goods and rights enshrined in the Thai Constitution.

7.9 Labour market information

There has been considerable debate on the structure, functions and location for a labour market information system centre or focal point. In order to decide on these issues and on a focal point, it is recommended that a working group be established with employers' organizations, workers' organisations, the Ministry of Labour and Social Welfare, the National Statistical Office, the National Economic and Social Development Board and the Thailand Development Research Institute as lead members. In the meantime, the Committee for Labour Force, Employment and Unemployment Estimation with the Department of Employment in the Ministry of Labour and Social Welfare would serve a coordinating role for disseminating statistics and preparing reports on the labour market.

Ongoing initiatives to improve labour statistics should be enhanced. Efforts should continue to improve the compilation of data from household-based surveys, establishment surveys and administrative records. These will serve to strengthen labour market information on the formal sector. The ILO has suggested ways in which major improvements might be effected in the conduct of establishment surveys. These surveys are especially important for the generation of reliable wage data. It is proposed that an informal sector survey be introduced to generate information for policy planning on this vital sector.

While the recent focus has been on the unemployment rate, a broader set of core labour market indicators is essential for active labour market policies. It is suggested that principal users of labour market information identify a key set of labour market indicators. Consultations with social partners indicate the following to be high priorities: labour slack, informal sector and micro-enterprises, income from employment, productivity and costs, internal migration and target groups. Wherever possible the data should be broken down by gender.

Data from Labour Force Surveys should be disaggregated to the extent possible to facilitate local-level planning. Links should be established at a local level between labour market information and other social statistics obtained from the Community Unemployment Register, the Labour Force Survey and other initiatives.

Enhancement of the capacity of government agencies and social partners to analyse, interpret and use labour market information is identified as the second area of priority. This requires a number of actions in the short and longer term. Within the Ministry of Labour and Social Welfare, a technical coordinating unit should be established. Its principal responsibilities would be to compile and analyse labour market information. This unit could produce the *Quarterly Labour Market Review* and carry out studies on selected labour and employment issues. It would serve as a coordinating unit and replace the fragmented system that now exists with technical studies and planning units in each department. The enhancement of capacity within the Ministry of Labour and Social Welfare for policy formulation and analysis of the labour market cannot be accomplished overnight and it requires a major programme of technical assistance.

References

Allal, Maurice. 1999. *Micro- and small enterprises in Thailand: Definitions and contributions*, Working paper 6 for the ILO/UNDP Project on Micro- and Small Enterprise Development and Poverty Alleviation in Thailand: THA/99/003 (Bangkok, ILO/EASMAT).

Areeya, Rojvithee. 1999. *Successful practices in HRD in the workplace: Contributions from labour, management and government, case studies from Thailand* (Bangkok, Department of skill Development, Ministry of Labour and Social Welfare, unpublished).

Bhatiasevi, A. 1999. "A health care scheme fails to help poor pregnant women", in *Bangkok Post*, 31 August 1999 (Bangkok).

Boonpratuang, C. 1999. *A review of action on employment relief*, NESDB paper presented at the ILO Asian Regional Consultation on Follow-up to the World Summit for Social Development (Bangkok, ILO/ROAP).

EIU (Economist Intelligence Unit). 1997. *Thailand, business operations report 4th Quarter 1997* (London).

———. 1999. *Country report, Thailand, 3rd quarter* (London).

Fraser, D. 1999. *The role of employment services in the management of the Thai labour market: A study of the recent past and possibilities for commencing the twenty-first century*, Report prepared for the MOLSW (Bangkok, ILO/EASMAT, unpublished).

Gosah Arya. 1999. *Economic crisis, employment and labour market in Thailand*, Report prepared for the ILO/EASMAT (Bangkok, unpublished).

Gray, Rossarin. 1999. *The effects of globalization on labour force and migration in Thailand*, Paper prepared for the Asia and Pacific Policy Seminar on the Impact of Globalization on Population Change and Poverty in Rural Areas (Bangkok, UN ESCAP).

Heller, P.S. 1999. *Human dimensions of the Asian economic crisis*, Paper prepared for the World Bank Regional Meeting on Social Issues Arising from the East Asia Crisis and Policy Implications for the Future (Washington D.C., Fiscal Affairs Department, IMF).

Hong, Tan; Geeta, Batra. 1995. *Enterprise training in developing countries: Incidence, productivity effects and policy implications* (Washington, D.C., World Bank).

ILO. 1993a. *Report of the conference*, 15th International Conference of Labour Statisticians (Geneva, International Labour Office).

———. 1993b. *Dynamism in the informal sector in a fast growing economy: The case of Bangkok* (New Delhi, ILO-ARTEP).

———. 1994. *Improving labour and social statistics in Thailand*, A report submitted to the Government of Thailand (Bangkok, ILO/EASMAT).

———. 1995a. *An enabling policy framework for urban informal sector* (Bangkok).

———. 1995b. *Thailand: Pensions and family benefits*, Report to the Government of Thailand on the development of social protection (Geneva, Social Security Department; Bangkok, ILO/EASMAT).

————. 1996. *Practical actions for the social protection of home-workers in Thailand* (Bangkok, ILO/ROAP).

————. 1997a. *Country briefing note: Thailand* (Bangkok, ILO-Bangkok Area Office, restricted).

————. 1997b. *Thailand at a crossroads*, Background paper for the Thailand-ILO National Tripartite Forum (Bangkok, ILO/EASMAT).

————. 1998a. *Thailand: Review of the social security scheme, Part II: Report on health insurance* (Geneva, Social Security Department, ILO/TF/Thailand/R36 (II)).

————. 1998b. *Thailand: Review of the social security scheme Part III: Report on the actuarial valuation of short-term benefits* (Geneva, Social Security Department, ILO/TF/Thailand/R36 (III)).

————. 1998c. *Thailand: Assessment of the feasibility of introducing an unemployment insurance scheme in Thailand*, Report to the Government (Geneva, Social Security Department).

————. 1999. *Wage policy and labour competitiveness in Thailand: Summary of main findings of phase one of the study and policy recommendations*, Report prepared for the MOLSW (Bangkok, ILO/EASMAT, unpublished draft).

ILO/AIT. 1998. *Gender, policy and the economic crisis* (Bangkok, ILO/ROAP, unpublished).

Kakwani, Nanak. 1998. *Impact of the economic crisis on employment, unemployment and real income* (Bangkok, NESDB and ADB).

Lall, S. 1998. *Thailand's manufacturing competitiveness: An overview*, in NESDB and the World Bank Thailand Office. *Competitiveness and sustainable economic recovery in Thailand*, Vol. 2: Background papers for the Conference on Thailand's Dynamic Economic Recovery and Competitiveness (Bangkok).

————. 1999. *Raising competitiveness in the Thai economy*, Paper prepared for the Thailand Country Employment Policy Review (Bangkok, ILO/EASMAT, unpublished).

Lee, Eddy. 1998. *The Asian financial crisis: The challenge for social policy* (Geneva, ILO).

Machida, S. 1999. *Programme of action for occupational safety and health in Thailand towards the twenty-first century: An advisory report* (Bangkok, ILO/EASMAT).

Mazumdar, Dipak. 1999. *Monitoring trends in the labour market*, Advisory paper prepared for the MOLSW (Bangkok, ILO/EASMAT).

Medhi, Krongkaew. 1997. *Poverty alleviation through public works: Cases of the Rural Job Creation Program, the Green Isarn Program, and the Tambon Development Programs*, Paper prepared for the World Bank (Bangkok, World Bank Office Thailand, unpublished).

Middleton, John; Tzannatos, Z. 1998. *Skills for competitiveness*, in NESDB/World Bank. *Competitiveness and sustainable economic recovery in Thailand*, Vol. 2: Background papers for the Conference on Thailand's Dynamic Economic Recovery and Competitiveness (Bangkok, NESDB and the World Bank Thailand Office).

Middleton, John; Nipon P.; Omporn R.; Chantavit S. 1991. *Vocational training in a changing economy – the case of Thailand* (Washington D.C., World Bank, working paper).

Department of Vocational Education, Ministry of Education. 1997. *Statistics* (Bangkok).

Ministry of Labour and Social Welfare, Thailand. 1998. *Yearbook of labour statistics, 1998* (Bangkok, Department of Labour Protection and Welfare).

————. 1998. *Skill development statistics, fiscal year 1997* (Bangkok, Department of Skill Development).

————. 1999. *Action plan to improve competitiveness of the labour force* (Bangkok, internal document).

Murray, Barbara. 1998. *Vocational training of disabled persons in Thailand: A challenge to policy-makers* (Bangkok, ILO/EASMAT).

Narong Petprasert. 1998. *Study of the public response to the employment impact of the financial crisis in Thailand* (Bangkok, CPES, Chulalongkorn University).

Nathan, D.; Kelkar, G.; Supanchaimat, N. 1998. *Carrying the burden of the crisis: Women and the rural poor in Thailand*, study prepared for the International Fund for Agricultural Development, cited in World Bank. 1999. *Thailand Social Monitor: Challenge for social reform* (Bangkok, Thailand World Bank Office).

National Economic and Social Development Board (NESDB), Thailand. 1995. *Population projections for Thailand, 1990-2020* (Bangkok, National Economic and Social Development Board).

————. 1998. *Indicators of well-being and policy analysis: in NESDB Newsletter*, Vol. 2, No. 4: *The impact of the economic crisis on the standard of living in Thailand* (Bangkok).

————. 1999. *Indicators of well-being and policy analysis, NESDB Newsletter*, Vol. 3, No. 2.

NESDB/World Bank. 1998. *Competitiveness and sustainable economic recovery in Thailand*, Vol. 2: Background papers for the Conference on Thailand's Dynamic Economic Recovery and Competitiveness (Bangkok, NESDB and the World Bank Thailand Office).

Niphon Phuaphongsakon and Yaowarat Sirwaranan. 1998. *Human Resource Data Centre Study, Supporting Document Set 8, A study for the purpose of preparing the Human Resource Development Master Plan of Thailand B.E. 2504-2549*, prepared for the Department of Skills Development, MOLSW (Bangkok, TDRI, unofficial English translation by ILO/EASMAT).

National Statistical Office (NSO), Thailand. 1996. *Formal and informal labour force market: Labour Force Survey, 1994* (Bangkok).

————. 1996. *Report of the 1995 business, trade and services survey – Whole Kingdom* (Bangkok).

————. 1998. *Report of the Labour Force Survey – Whole Kingdom*, Round 3, August 1998 (Bangkok).

———. 1998. *Report of the 1996 listing of industrial and business establishments – Whole Kingdom* (Bangkok).

Pember, Robert. 1997. *Statistical monitoring of the labour market* (Bangkok, ILO/EASMAT, internal document).

———. 1998. *Improvements to the system of establishment-based surveys in Thailand*, (Bangkok, ILO/EASMAT, internal document).

Pyke, F. 1998. *Small firms, industrial relations and new roles for employers' and workers' organizations*, Background paper for the 1997-98 World Labour Report (Geneva, ILO).

Santosh, Mehrotra. 1998. *Mitigating the social impact of the economic crisis: A review of the Royal Thai Government's response*, Paper prepared for UNICEF (New York).

Sungsidh Piriyarangsan. 1998. *Bipartite systems: Workplace relations in Thailand*, Report prepared for ILO/EASMAT (Bangkok).

Sununta Siengthai. 1999. *Industrial relations and the recession in Thailand*, Report prepared for the Thailand Country employment Policy Review (Bangkok, ILO/EASMAT).

TDRI. 1998. *Human resource development plan for Thailand's manufacturing and service industry 1997-2006*, Report prepared for the Department of Skills Development (Bangkok, TDRI, unofficial English translation by ILO/EASMAT).

Theeravit N. 1999. *Towards gender equality at work in Thailand*, Report prepared for ILO/EASMAT (Bangkok, ILO/EASMAT, unpublished).

Tzannatos, Z. 1997. *Growth and inequality in Thailand: An overview of labour market issues*, Draft 1 (Washington D.C., World Bank, unpublished).

UNDP. 1997. *Human development report 1997* (New York, Oxford University Press).

———. 1999. *Common Country Assessment for Thailand* (Bangkok, UN Resident Coordinator System, UNDP).

World Bank. 1996. *Thailand: growth, poverty and income distribution: An economic report*, No. 15689-TH 1996 (Country Operations Division, Country Department I, East Asia and Pacific Region).

———. 1999. *Thailand Social Monitor: Challenge for social reform* (Bangkok, World Bank Thailand Office).

World Bank, Thailand; Office of the National Education Commission. 1999. *Secondary and vocational education in Thailand, moving towards 12 years for all: A study of policy options* (Bangkok).

Yongyuth Chalamwong; Sakdina Sontisakyotin; Napapan Meepadung. 1999. *Improvements in policy formulation through improved Thailand Labour Force Surveys*, Paper prepared for ILO/EASMAT (Bangkok, TDRI).

Zeufack, Albert G. 1999. *Employer-provided training under oligopolistic labour markets* (Washington D.C., World Bank).

List of acronyms

ADB	Asian Development Bank
AIT	Asian Institute of Technology
ARTEP	Asian Regional Team for Employment Promotion, International Labour Office
ASEAN	Association of South East Asian Nations
AUSAID	Australian Agency for International Development
BAO	Bangkok Area Office
CCA	Common Country Assessment
CEPR	Country Employment Policy Review
CPES	Centre for Political Economy Studies, Chulalongkorn University
DIP	Department of Industrial Promotion, Ministry of Industry
DOVE	Department of Vocational Education, Ministry of Education, Royal Thai Government
DSD	Department of Skill Development, Ministry of Labour and Social Welfare, Royal Thai Government
EASMAT	East Asia Multidisciplinary Advisory Team, International Labour Office
ECONTHAI	Employers' Confederation of Thai Trade and Industry
EIU	Economist Intelligence Unit
ESCAP	Economic and Social Commission for Asia and the Pacific, United Nations
GDP	Gross Domestic Product
GNP	Gross National Product
HRD	Human Resource Development
IBRD	International Bank for Reconstruction and Development (World Bank)
ICFTU	International Confederation of Free Trade Unions
ICFTU-APRO	International Confederation of Free Trade Unions – Asian and Pacific Regional Organisation
IFAD	International Fund for Agricultural Development
ILO	International Labour Organization
IMF	International Monetary Fund
ISCED	International Standards Classification of Education
ISO	International Organization for Standardization
KILM	Key Indicators of the Labour Market
LCT	Labour Congress of Thailand
LMI	Labour Market Information
MoE	Ministry of Education, Royal Thai Government
MOLSW	Ministry of Labour and Social Welfare, Royal Thai Government
NCTL	National Congress of Thai Labour
NESDB	National Economic and Social Development Board, Royal Thai Government
NGO	Non-Governmental Organization
NLDAC	National Labour Development Advisory Council
NSO	National Statistical Office, Office of the Prime Minister, Royal Thai Government

NVTCC	National Vocational Training Coordination Committee
ONEC	Office of the National Education Commission
OUP	Oxford University Press
PES	Public Employment Service
POLEMP	ILO Employment and Labour Market Policies Branch
R&D	Research and Development
RMCS	Regional Model Competency Standards
ROAP	Regional Office for Asia and the Pacific, International Labour Office
SERC	State Enterprise Workers' Relations Confederation
SIP	Social Investment Programme
SME	Small and Medium-sized Enterprise
SMI	Small and Medium-sized Industry
SOE	State-owned Enterprise
SSO	Social Security Office
SPPD	Support Services to Policy and Programme Development
SSPL	Social Sector Programme Loan
TDRI	Thailand Development Research Institute
TVE	Technical and Vocational Education
UN	United Nations
UNDP	United Nations Development Programme
UNESCO	United Nations Educational, Scientific and Cultural Organization
UNICEF	United Nations Children's Fund
VT	Vocational Training